ELIZABETH BOYD

Already Forgiven

An Abortion Recovery Story

PLATYPUS
PUBLISHING

First published by Platypus Publishing 2024

Copyright © 2024 by Elizabeth Boyd

All rights reserved. No part of this publication may be reproduced, stored or transmitted in any form or by any means, electronic, mechanical, photocopying, recording, scanning, or otherwise without written permission from the publisher. It is illegal to copy this book, post it to a website, or distribute it by any other means without permission.

Elizabeth Boyd asserts the moral right to be identified as the author of this work.

Elizabeth Boyd has no responsibility for the persistence or accuracy of URLs for external or third-party Internet Websites referred to in this publication and does not guarantee that any content on such Websites is, or will remain, accurate or appropriate.

First edition

ISBN: 978-1-962133-41-8

This book was professionally typeset on Reedsy. Find out more at reedsy.com

This book is dedicated to all the unborn children and to the parents who must carry on without them.

Contents

Preface	ii
Acknowledgement	iv
Introduction	v
1 Shadows In My Past	1
2 Thailand	16
3 The Darkest Night Of My Soul	26
4 Consequences	29
5 Good Grief	39
6 Support	44
7 The Deepest Longing Of My Heart	53
8 Miracles	56
9 Infinite Possibility	61
10 Re-Knowing Myself	66
11 Climbing Mountains	74
12 Grace	80
Afterword	86
Grace's Quilt	89
Resources	90
About the Author	91

Preface

"The wound is the place where the Light enters you."
— Rumi

After the devastation I felt resulting from an abortion experience, I discovered that resources to help people recover from such a trauma were slim at best and not easy to find. I worked through a lot of pain with minimal guidance and support to find a way to feel at peace with my past. I wrote this book for my own healing. I am no expert in trauma recovery, but over the years I figured out a lot of things as I went from hurt to healed. I gained knowledge and tools that helped me come to terms with my experience.

I read one woman's story about her abortion experiences and didn't find it particularly helpful in a practical sense. It was largely faith-based and passive. It was comforting to know that she had healed emotionally after an abortion, but I still didn't know how to find this elusive healing. I realized that, more than faith alone, I needed to take action. But what action? I started with the most obvious thing I could think of, which was counseling, and then followed the breadcrumbs. One thing led to another, and so on and so forth. When I finally reached a place of healing I looked back at my journey. I mentally reverse-engineered every action I had taken and every phase I had passed. In doing this, I noticed that there were specific necessary steps that I took, which allowed me to reach a place that finally feels like peace.

I will admit that prior to having an abortion I judged those who would resort to abortion and I judged abortion itself. After I found myself in a situation that led me to choose abortion, I could no longer judge it or anyone who would consider it. Personally it was the worst decision I could make for myself and therefore the trauma of it followed and haunted me. When I finally realized that writing a book would aid my healing I felt scared to share my secret, but I reluctantly started putting my story down on paper. The more I wrote the easier it became, and an entire story poured out of my wounds....

Acknowledgement

First I give huge thanks to my husband Jay. He allowed me to feel safe by giving me space to feel sad on the days when the subject matter of my writing was particularly heavy. Without a safe space to write, I don't know how I could ever have shared my story.

Next, my deepest gratitude goes to my beta readers Donna Miller, Sandi Duverneuil, "Auntie" Claudia Ringgold Rueb, Naomi Mori, Diane Morrell, Luisa Giacometti, Christine Matamoros, and Andrea Lippke. Their profound insights showed me where I could make changes that would improve the quality of the reader's experience. Based on their feedback I filled in some gaps and added more context. I even overhauled a couple of sections and rewrote them completely. Indeed, this is a different book than the one my friends first read, and, dare I say, it's better.

Finally, I thank Grace whose invisible but constant presence motivated and spurred me on through the roller coaster of emotions that I felt throughout this project. I have never felt so much love through so much pain as I reflected on all the ways that its presence touched my life and forever changed me. Grace made this process feel both bitter and sweet, like the true love story that it is.

Introduction

"I'd like to try abortion one day," said no one ever.

* * *

Turning to abortion at the age of eighteen is the biggest mistake I've ever made in my life. I truly wanted that baby, and I thought I'd never forgive myself for what I did. It destroyed me inside, and somehow I thought I deserved to endure the pain of it for decades. I felt ashamed of my past. I didn't believe I could talk freely about my abortion decision. I felt I must forever carry my burden alone. It required immense healing and yet I found very little guidance on how to heal.

We all make mistakes. In fact, we're supposed to make mistakes so we can learn through them. I think the hope is that we can learn enough from small mistakes that we don't need to make big ones, but even so, we sometimes still call impossibly big lessons to our experience.

"I'm a smart person and I'm a good person who made ONE bad decision. Why the hell can't I heal? What am I missing?"

Those were the questions I asked myself twenty years after making the regrettable choice to terminate my first pregnancy. Okay, so I messed up. Feeling badly made sense on one level, but I couldn't accept that I should remain stuck feeling miserably for the rest of my life. I refused to believe that it was my lot to heal only ninety percent of the way from a poor decision and live the rest of my life still suffering that final ten percent. I know people who have healed from their abortion experiences. I was doing all the things they had done. I had come a long way, but I was stuck. I felt like my healing had plateaued. Feeling desperate, I started saying a daily prayer. "Help me to release that which no longer serves." I needed help. I needed more than help. I needed a miracle.

Then one day I randomly saw an advertisement on Facebook for a program called Your Year of Miracles (YOM) led by Marci Shimoff, Dr. Sue Morter, and Lisa Garr. It grabbed my attention so I signed up for one of the free live masterclasses. On a December morning, between dropping my children off for school and grocery shopping, I listened intently as Marci and Dr. Sue explained that miracles are something we not only deserve, but which we should expect. Apparently, it was possible to create the right conditions for miracles to show up regularly. I needed to learn how to do this. There, in the parking lot outside the Natural Grocers in Hurst, Texas, I enrolled in the upcoming Your Year of Miracles program for 2019.

I had no idea what to expect, but on that December day I opened myself up to the possibility that the miracle of my total and complete healing was available to me. For perhaps the first time ever, I allowed myself to stop wanting to heal. Instead I started believing that healing was mine. I still had no idea how to heal fully, but somehow Marci and Dr. Sue helped instill within me a faith that I had previously lacked. I felt a spring of joy and inner peace welling up inside me. For the rest of that day I walked on clouds.

Then, before we even had our first live YOM call for the year, my biggest miracle occurred. On the 12th of January, while attending a workshop, I fainted for no apparent reason. When I came to, I was a different person. I was at peace with my past. Something inside me had changed fundamentally. What exactly changed and how?

Through this experience I learned about forgiveness, self-love, and, of course, miracles. I stopped hating and judging myself for what I had done and started learning all the ways to love myself. My new perspective allowed me to see myself and others through a completely different lens. I learned how to tell a new story about an old event.

I did, in fact, learn how to create the right conditions for miracles to show up regularly in my life. The miracles, big and small, keep pouring in to this day. The writing of this book itself is nothing short of a miracle. I never wanted to stand out or be noticed in any big way. To broadcast something that I had kept secret for 20 years is disconcerting, to say the least ... but that's something I learned about miracles. They don't always show up how you hope or expect they will. When I started daily receiving an impulse to write a book my first reactions were, "I don't want to write a book" and "I don't know how." Then I realized that the book was the final piece of the puzzle. Facing my fears and publicly sharing my mistake would set me down a path from which I can no longer hide—the path of complete healing.

I have written this book because I have some big karma to untangle. When I had an abortion I hurt myself more than any human alive could possibly have hurt me because the truth is that I wanted to be a mother. I wanted my baby. My decision to abort my first child plunged me into 10 years of depression. After that I spent another 10 years attempting to heal from the abortion.

When I finally started seeking healing I looked in all the right places—the church, the Bible, friends, self-help books ... but I wasn't getting that much better. The problem wasn't where I was trying to get help. It was that I was expecting something outside myself to heal me when the truth is that healing is an inside job. I wanted all these people, things, and organizations to "fix" me. I had no idea, firstly, that there was nothing to "fix" because there was never anything wrong with me and, secondly, that no one could ever heal me because I had to heal myself.

It's natural and necessary to find and utilize good help, but any outside assistance, whether it's scripture or your sister, is just a band-aid.

There's a perfect time and a place for a band-aid. It covers and cocoons a wound so that no new dirt enters while it heals inside. My problem is that I got confused. I repeatedly mistook the band-aid for the remedy. I may as well have plastered band-aids all over my body and strutted around like a walking billboard for "healing." I was stuck in the rut of my story—always healing, never healed. I knew the pain so well that I didn't see how to *un*-know it. Today I understand that it's good to put a band-aid on ... and even better to rip it off.

When I finally healed, the following things were true. First, and most importantly, my healing, *no matter the cost*, became non-negotiable. I stopped hiding from the work. I rolled up my sleeves and prepared to get my hands dirty. Second, I accepted responsibility for the abortion and stopped judging myself for it. There was nothing wrong with my mess. It was both ugly *and* perfect, and I could use it to learn a new way of healing. Third, healing is not passive, so I found the support that showed me what to do and how to apply the healing work in my actual life. Fourth, I learned not only to believe in miracles but to expect them. I learned that I could create the conditions for miracles to show up for me, including in the form of my own healing.

No one is broken beyond repair. Healing is for everyone. It just takes perseverance, a little creativity, and a lot of elbow grease.

People say that time heals. Well that's not true. It's what we do with the time that leads to any healing. Time only allows us the space we require to do the healing work and then integrate that healing into our being so that we can feel it and the people around us can see it.

When I finally ripped off my emotional band-aids and got to work, a healing process unfolded for me. It was often clumsy and it was completely based on trial and error, but it resulted in peace with my past when I learned how to rewire my brain. It was only in hindsight as I contemplated all the twisted paths I had traveled that I realized I had followed a formula. I'm sharing that formula now in the way it revealed itself to me. Sometimes I still have a hard time understanding how something so simple could change my life 180 degrees. All I know is I went from pain to peace almost overnight. If something so easy could work for me then there's a chance it just might help others too. I hope one of those people is you.

1

Shadows In My Past

"Of all the liars in the world, sometimes the worst are our own fears."
—Rudyard Kipling

In order to start at the beginning, I have to address that age old antagonist called fear. Through the course of our lifetimes, we all inevitably develop our own unique sets of fears. Some people don't seem to be scared of much, while others seem to be scared of everything. I think I fell somewhere on the heavily scared end of that spectrum. At least, the things that I feared felt deeply scary and therefore it was traumatic when I experienced them.

I was painfully shy as a child. Some of my earliest memories are of feeling terrified of strangers. They didn't even have to be total strangers. Relatives who we didn't see often fell into the category of strangers and therefore felt unsafe to me. I remember wanting to bury my face in my mother's leg, rather than look at anyone I didn't know. Worse than looking, I turned to stone when asked to speak a word to anyone outside my closest family. I remember the sensation of flushing hot, terrified and embarrassed when I managed to choke out a greeting at the coaxing of an adult. I wanted to want to talk. I really did. It just felt so completely terrifying that I felt like crying instead.

The only thing that might have scared me more than humans was dogs. For a shy introvert such as myself, the energy of a dog was far too much to handle. The slobbering, disgusting mouths, greasy shedding coats, and booming barks of these no-mannered food thieves crossed absolutely every boundary I had. As a small child, not much taller than a dog, I felt completely violated when one of these domestic beasts would shove its nose in my face, sniffing and prodding me on the greeting and mercilessly whipping me with its tail on its retreat. I felt so completely defenseless when a dog would jump up on me that I couldn't understand why anyone would invite one of these animals into their life, let alone their home. I saw so many people around me enjoying the company of dogs that I wished I liked dogs. As I got older I even remember copying my friends who had dogs in an attempt to be like them and force myself to like dogs. If my friends hugged their dog, I would hug their dog. If my friends threw a ball for their dog to chase, then I would wrangle the ball from its mouth and toss it. Unfortunately, nothing ever helped me warm up to dogs, and the only thing I ever accomplished was judging myself for not liking dogs. At least, as I grew taller, I no longer felt afraid of them.

From preschool through high school, the institution of school presented a huge challenge to me. I didn't want a spotlight shone on me in any way. I was afraid to do anything in large groups. I didn't want to be observed, judged, or corrected. I didn't want to raise my hand in class, even when I knew the right answer. What if my right answer was actually wrong? What if I said something that I thought was intelligent but was actually stupid? What if I said something that I thought was normal but my classmates had no idea what I was talking about? I didn't want to talk during class, period.

I was downright afraid of being wrong. I didn't know how to handle it if I gave a "wrong" answer in class. I would blush hot pink while my body temperature shot through the roof. Worse yet, I actually did pretty well in school most of the time. Since I was known for being "smart," my classmates would open their eyes incredulously and gape at me with open mouths if I gave a wrong answer out loud in class. It was utterly humiliating and it made me not want to participate at all, even when I knew that I knew the correct answer. It's not that I never raised my hand to answer a question, but sometimes my arm felt like a lead weight, impossible to lift.

I felt daily anxiety in school. Forget academics. I never felt like I fit in socially. Sure, I had friends, but I somehow didn't talk the way they talked or wear the clothes they wore, or style my hair in the current fashion like they did. At lunch I had weird "healthy" food to eat and I ate too slowly to finish before lunch ended and recess began.

Grades were the worst. As I mentioned, I was a good student. By that I mean I usually got high grades. In the fourth grade is when they started assigning letter grades to our homework and the tests we took. All of a sudden, I didn't feel okay if I scored anything lower than a B+ on anything. Most of the time that wasn't a problem, but there were areas that I had to work harder than others to achieve that A. Math and science didn't come as naturally to me as reading or spelling. Social studies and history were a toss up because they were very interesting but quite complex and I often got wrapped up in the story of it all while somehow missing the details that showed up on the test. The result is that, over the years, I started having to sit with my homework for increasingly longer periods of time in order to keep my grades high. After all, I had set a standard early on. I couldn't stand the shame of dropping below a high B. How would I manage people's criticism of me? I imagined their voices in my head. "She's so smart. I wonder what's going on?" "It isn't like her to get a mediocre grade." Teachers do their best to push their students. Unfortunately, conventional teachers in a conventional educational system use grades as benchmarks of their students' progress and success. My teachers had only the best of intentions when encouraging my "good" grades. They saw the results of my natural ability and couldn't see the insecurity underneath it. I drove myself crazy not even knowing that the person judging me the most harshly was myself. What if I had allowed myself to ease up a bit with the homework and the studying? What if I had gotten plain B's or, better yet, a C? Of course if I had adjusted my output everyone around me would have adjusted their expectations over time, but I couldn't ever see that as a possibility.

My sister who was just a grade behind me in school was also bright and also did well in school. Monica is fifteen months younger than I am, so teachers had me in class one year and Monica the next. Early on, I began comparing myself to Monica. She got excellent grades, so of course I worked to keep my grades high. If she scored higher than I had on a project from the previous year, I wondered if I could have done better. In fact, I believed I absolutely should have done better. Our parents naturally loved that their daughters were so studious and performed well in school. Parents can relax when teachers enjoy having their child in class. If your child is doing so well, what can be wrong? What more must you do as a parent? All the signals would tend to suggest that absolutely nothing is wrong and that they shouldn't change a thing. Therefore, I never heard the words, "I'm glad you're consistently achieving high scores, but we don't care about your grades. Grades aren't you. How are *you* feeling?" I never heard anything like that, at least not strongly enough that it actually resonated. All that I had were my own thoughts and no one wise enough or aware enough to guide them.

As scared as I was to get low grades, I was equally afraid of sinning. I was raised in the Catholic faith and from first through twelfth grade I attended Catholic schools. I learned many things about the nature of love and all its aspects that serve me well to this day, but I also learned about sin and what not to do according to the Catholic church. This girl who already had a habit of being scared to do anything wrong, who already had a habit of judging herself over something as arbitrary as grades, learned all about how to do things "right" in order to avoid being judged by the church. With all my natural anxiety, it might seem like following the strict rules of the Catholic church posed too heavy a burden to bear. Fortunately for me, we all know that copious amounts of fear and stress set people up for great success! (Yes, this comment drips with sarcasm.)

Growing up I always felt "weird." Our family was not the "typical" American family, and I felt very alienated because of this. We weren't allowed to eat red meat. We weren't allowed to eat sugar. We rarely received toys or other gifts if it wasn't our birthday or Christmas. We weren't allowed to watch most movies or TV shows beyond a "G" rating. When we children were old enough to drive we weren't allowed to buy our own car. We weren't allowed to ride in a car on the highway when a friend was driving. I felt embarrassed, constantly explaining to friends that I couldn't do this or eat that. Of course they always asked why. It was downright exhausting trying to explain all the reasons when deep down I wished all those reasons would just disappear so I could be "normal."

Our family motto could have been "the cheaper the better." As a family of seven we were understandably on a tight, no-frills budget. My parents made a decision early on to prioritize saving money, both for their future needs and for their children's education. I am forever grateful that they taught me the practicality of saving money, but the extreme ways that we did without came at a real cost to my perception of my own self worth.

I remember feeling uncomfortable even in my own home. When I was thirteen, my parents had a new house built, which appeared grand and beautiful on the outside, but which soon started to feel dingy and disjointed on the inside. In my room my sister and I had built-in desks that never received chairs. I desperately wanted a chair, but instead I hauled a bar stool upstairs and downstairs each day that I sat at my desk to do homework. At one point my dad removed the three incandescent bulbs in my bedroom light fixture only to replace them with a single fluorescent bulb that popped and sputtered in protest every time someone turned it on. Even when it warmed up fully, I always felt as if I were straining my eyes to read at night. Then there were the showers. My dad replaced each shower head in the house with a nozzle with a switch that could reduce the flow of water when we didn't need a full stream. In quasi-military style, the routine was turn on full stream, wet body, reduce stream, put in shampoo, return to full stream, rinse shampoo.... You get the idea.

As bad as those showers were, each winter brought the worst insult of all when, rather than pay for adequate heating, we would shiver with cold inside our own home. In California's central coast it doesn't snow during the winter, but overnight temperatures can reach freezing at the coldest times of the year. We kept our heater on a timer. It would turn on briefly each morning while we got ready for school or work. All other times we lit a fire in a single pellet stove downstairs in the family room. Incidentally, we only allowed our central heat to remain on all day for Christmas and for New Year when we would be hosting family, which obviously meant that the comfort of others was way more important than my own.

Living through winters on heat rations is absolutely do-able. This is a normal experience for a lot of people. All I can say is it was not pleasant to know that we had the means to be warm and purposefully chose not to use them. I remember nights staying up late working on homework wrapped in blankets to insulate me from the freezing air inside our home. On more than one occasion, I sat typing a report for a school project with fingers so icy cold that they could barely move across a keyboard properly. One cold winter afternoon while my parents were both out, my sister Monica turned up the heat. For a couple of wonderful hours we enjoyed the strange sensation of feeling comfortably warm inside our house. When our dad returned home to the electricity bill being shot through the roof, Monica found herself on the receiving end of his angry, harsh words. Rather than get yelled at all the time, we learned to survive in the cold.

For some reason my family didn't get to have nice things. We typically bought things second-hand rather than new. I also observed that when something broke or wore down in our home, we often didn't replace or fix it. Could we do without it? Could we work around it not functioning properly? If the answer was yes, then we put no effort into repair or replacement. Do you remember the bar stools that I carried upstairs and downstairs between my desk and the kitchen bar? When those bar stool legs started breaking, my dad zip tied the legs together. It was one hundred percent function and zero percent style. Over the years, the sun streaming through the sliding glass doors burned the linoleum floor in the family room. We lived with a growing patch of gross discoloration and an eventual large hole in the linoleum. The upholstery on the sofa wore thin. We ignored it for years. Eventually one section of a multi-section sofa would receive a slipcover that didn't match the rest of the sofa. My life painted a vivid picture for me that not only were my feelings unimportant, but no one in my family was important. I grew up in a mental and emotional state of lack.

There are five children in our family and only eight and a half years between myself and the youngest. From my perspective as the oldest, it always seemed like it was more necessary for the adults in my life to tend the younger children than to check in and spend time with me. I didn't even know to question or resent this. To compound matters, I grew up next door to my cousin Rose. She is only three months younger than I am and an only child. We attended school together for twelve years. I sometimes enjoyed spending time with Rose, but often she treated me poorly. My mom expected me to behave graciously and share my things, even when I didn't want to. Rose, on the other hand, was quite spoiled and had a very hard time with sharing and nearly always got her way. She included lying, cheating, biting, and scratching in her repertoire of manipulations to control my sisters and me. She was a bully who wasn't afraid to use her skills. Even when Rose was downright mean to the point that I told an adult, she rarely (to my knowledge) received any consequences or punishment from either my parents or hers. I felt like the subject of a capricious tyrant who would invite me to play with her one moment, then snatch all the toys away the next. I remember one time Rose brought her Game Boy to our house. I never owned a Game Boy and I wanted a turn to play Super Mario Brothers on it. Rose said I could play when she was finished. I eagerly watched her make Mario jump, dodge enemies, and collect coins, trying my best to memorize the moves that would keep me alive in the game. After Rose had satiated her desire to manipulate Mario, she opened up the back of the Game Boy and checked the batteries. "The batteries are hot," she declared. "I need to turn it off."

Rose never turned that Game Boy back on while she was at our house. This type of scenario repeated itself in various different iterations over and over throughout the course of my childhood. I developed a dysfunctional relationship regarding things I wanted and how I got them. My entire childhood, an unkind person seemed to hold all the power and own all the cool stuff. If I wanted access to any of these things I had to play by her rules. If I were lucky, I might get a few minutes with a Game Boy or other high-ticket item. Growing up with this double standard felt terribly confusing and hurt me deeply. The fact that my parents never stood up for me drove home the subtle message that what I wanted must not be important. Deeper still, I myself must not be important.

There was one particular incident that finally drove the nail in the coffin of my feelings, so to speak. I was fifteen. I decided to visit my friend who lived a couple of houses down from us with her large family. When I arrived, only her father was home. He invited me in and offered me a glass of water. I was always friendly with him and his family. I sat for a bit on the couch, sipped water, and made small talk about school, my family, and the weather. Then I excused myself to leave. He joked, "Don't go." I laughed at the joke and headed to the door. At the front door he hugged me goodbye but—wait a moment. What was happening? He was holding me too tightly. He wasn't letting me go! He kissed my neck several times as I said "stop" over and over and finally pushed him away. Thank goodness he didn't fight me too hard. With effort I pulled myself out of his strong embrace and ran home.

I plunged into a depression. For months I told no one what happened. I wasn't accustomed to anyone sharing anything deeply personal in our family. I had no idea whom I could confide in. In fact, the thought of telling anyone what our neighbor had done felt scarier than carrying the shame and confusion I was feeling. I felt violated, lonely, lost, and unsafe. I withdrew as much as possible from my family. I would come home from school and immediately go to my room to do my homework. I would only go downstairs for dinner and then return upstairs for more homework and then to sleep. My mother knew something was wrong, but I didn't feel comfortable sharing with her. We weren't a family that discussed things like emotions or personal topics. I felt miserable and couldn't figure out how to escape the despair I felt. Only after several months, when I was desperate to feel better, did I finally get up the courage to tell my mom about the incident with our neighbor.

My mom set up appointments for me with the school counselor and bought me a bottle of a women's multivitamin supplement, as suggested by the counselor. She ultimately preferred to leave the past alone. We barely talked about it. Was I okay now? Yes. (I wasn't really okay, but

I didn't know that.) We didn't confront our neighbor. We didn't file a police report. I remember thinking that I didn't want to do anything to hurt our neighbor or his family. After all, they were our friends. I didn't understand that it's okay to report abuse even though reporting it might make someone uncomfortable. I know now that I have a right not to be violated. I know now that I have a right to feel safe. Unfortunately, my mom couldn't teach me these things. I had hoped my mother would point me in the right direction or at least make me feel better. Instead I felt worse. I felt let down, helpless, and alone. I wasn't important. I wasn't worthy. I wasn't safe.

It's never easy or obvious to uncover what's at the root of a feeling. It took me years to understand that I felt unimportant. The difficulty for me was that I've always liked myself. I had no idea that I could like myself without loving myself. To me it seemed as though "like" and "love" went hand in hand.

I have always run a terrific survival narrative in my head. It's so good that I had myself fooled for decades. Basically, I'm a happy optimist by nature. I have always been able to find the bright side of a situation easily. Unfortunately, my optimism blinded me to my own low sense of self-worth. People could treat me poorly, and instead of standing up for myself I would look through my optimist's lens and take on a sense of martyrdom that somehow substituted for self-esteem. "It's for the greater good," I told myself more times than I care to remember. I fully believed that the bully or abuser must require my peaceful, passive, example. In other words, it was the right thing to allow others to put me down or walk over me because it was serving a higher good.

I have painted a picture of growing up feeling scared, isolated, and unworthy. I have also talked about how I felt like I was told "no" more often than I was told "yes." In fact, the only easy "yes" I remember receiving was permission to travel. During high school my church became associated with an organization in Tijuana, Mexico called

Esperanza which means "hope" in English. They coordinated an annual trip for a week each year in Tijuana. This trip was open to anyone to join. Those who participated would help build houses for poor families during the week they spent in Tijuana. All through high school I studied Spanish. Because I loved Spanish and I loved traveling, this sounded like a perfect opportunity for me. I went on two mission trips to Tijuana, Mexico at fifteen and again at eighteen years old. I also had a really big adventure during the summer when I was seventeen when I spent six weeks in Barcelona, Spain studying Spanish. I had always desired to travel, and I learned that the only big thing I was allowed to do was travel. My time in Tijuana and Barcelona are some of my best memories from my high school years. I started to feel like only when I traveled far away from home was I free. I was a "good" girl who was too scared to be "bad." I had spent my entire life thus far being what I thought I was supposed to be. By the end of high school I could only say three things for certain about myself: 1. I wanted to travel a lot. 2. I loved studying foreign languages. 3. I wanted to get married and have children.

As I approached the age of eighteen, I imagined that becoming a legal adult would somehow flip a switch. Life would become easy and the world would start to say "yes!" After all the denial I experienced through childhood, becoming an adult in the eyes of the law looked like a gateway to some magical land of opportunity.

There are only so many times a person can be told she can't do something before hitting the breaking point. I had to run away. College was on the horizon, but a bigger idea was brewing in my head. I would be entering college with an entire semester's worth of credit earned by passing multiple AP exams. I could take some time off and travel to Thailand. I had gone to Prom with a Thai exchange student named Win, and we started dating right after that. I had a job at a bank and saved most of the money I earned. I could live with Win and his family. I could stay for six months before I had to return and resume my studies.

Via letters in the mail I asked for Win's family's permission to live with them from December of 1998 through June of 1999. They agreed. I asked my parents' permission to travel to Thailand for six months. They didn't think it was a good idea, and there was no discussion about it. I couldn't take it any more. It was the last "no." It was the proverbial straw that broke the camel's back.

I entered California State University Monterey Bay as a student in the Fall of 1998. Sundays through Thursdays I lived on campus, and the remaining days I returned home to Hollister where I worked at a local Bank of America branch every weekend. One particular Friday morning, I arranged to drop my mom off at the school in Hollister where she taught. As soon as the nearby travel agency opened I walked in with my checkbook in hand and sat down in front of an agent. She searched for round trip flights to Bangkok from San Francisco with dates six months apart. My hand shook like an earthquake as I wrote that check, and my heart sat in my stomach when the agent handed me my freshly printed plane ticket to Thailand.

A new woman emerged from the travel agency that day. I was still a shy and scared girl at heart, but I had finally made a bold move. I sat in the car a moment before starting the engine. I will never forget the song that played—"Snow on the Sahara" by Anggun. In her beautifully hypnotic voice, Anggun pleaded with me, "Only tell me that you still want me here when you wander off out there ..." Would anyone here say that to me? I knew that Win wanted me. The song went on to say, "If that's the only place where you can leave your doubts I'll hold you up and be your way out ..." That sounded exactly like the support I wanted! I wanted someone to beg me not to leave while also assure me that if I must go they would help me no matter what. "And if we burn away, I'll pray the skies above for snow to fall on the Sahara ..." Someone please have my back, and if I completely fail to find what I seek, and I'm destroying myself in the process, then pray for the miracle that will save me. I allowed myself to take in the song—the music, the lyrics, and the vibration. In that moment it seemed like this song must be playing specifically for me.

I felt incredibly nervous about telling my parents that I had bought a plane ticket to Thailand against their wishes. After my mom's day at the school was over, I returned to pick her up. While she finished straightening up the classroom I gathered my courage and finally blurted out something that resembled, "Mom, I have some news. I bought a plane ticket to Thailand."

For how nervous I had felt to tell my mom, her response to this information was completely underwhelming. It was not much more than a limp, "You did?" She listened to me tell her the logistical details. Mom didn't have a lot of questions and, once again, there was no discussion. She stoically accepted that I had made my own decision and resigned herself to whatever that meant. I think my dad put up a little more resistance to my plan later that evening, but he didn't fight hard.

To go from a strict upbringing to the feeling of all boundaries suddenly and completely being withdrawn was a strange sensation. A big part of me exclaimed, "Finally!" Another part of me wondered what planet my parents had visited and when they would return. Did they care about me? Did they even understand what was happening?

Growing up I never got a lot of push back from my parents in most regards. If they didn't want me to do something I got a strong and final "no." I rarely got the opportunity to earn a "yes." I was so good at obeying that they didn't get much practice disciplining me or negotiating the terms differently. I remember actually wanting to be grounded when I was about twelve or thirteen years old. I would hear about my classmates being grounded by their parents for misbehaving and it sounded so cool. I must have been way too easy on my parents!

I always wanted to feel some resistance from my parents, but I didn't want to have to be "bad" in order to get big attention from them. One day I thought I had a brilliant idea to get some push back from my parents without misbehaving. I was in sixth grade. The most awesome thing about being in sixth grade was that we got to go away to science camp for several days in the Santa Cruz mountains. I was very excited for this trip away from my family ... and secretly very excited for family night—the one evening that the families could come have dinner with the campers. I thought I was so clever and cute. With a coy smile, I teased my parents on multiple occasions about how I did *not* want them to visit me at science camp. Of course I knew that they would show up anyway. They always supported me if it was related to school.

Not everyone's family could attend family night. When the day arrived, I rolled my eyes to my friends and said, "My parents will definitely be here," feigning annoyance. That evening we all headed to the dining hall for dinner. As parents started arriving, I excitedly sneaked glances at the door. Family after family entered. I knew that mine would be here any minute. More families arrived. That was strange. My family was running a bit later than I had expected. After a while the flow of guests stopped. Either my family was incredibly late or they actually weren't coming. I couldn't believe it.

I ate dinner that evening at a table with other friends whose families could not make it. As dinner wrapped up my best friend commented,

"Hey, I thought your family was coming."

"I thought they were, too," I replied.

Even though I had set myself up for this exact situation with all the teasing not to come see me, I felt sad, confused, and let down.

I came from a passive family culture. We didn't fight. We didn't debate. If we disagreed, we kept quiet. We communicated the most when all parties were in agreement. My parents never asked me why I wouldn't want them to come visit me at science camp. They took my word at face value and didn't show up. Now years later, my parents weren't going to ask me what plans I had for visiting Thailand. They just accepted the fact that I was going.

It sounds strange to want conflict, but everyone needs some solid lines to know where the boundaries are. Healthy arguments and debate help people know who they are and where they stand as well as understand the people and the world around them. Children growing up need to know that they are loved enough to have certain limits enforced but also respected enough that they can push those limits and be met with thoughtful, productive dialogue. Children need to feel heard and validated. At eighteen, I had no idea if my parents could hear me. I knew they loved me, but I had no idea if they actually knew what I wanted or cared about what I needed. That's why I had to run away to know myself. I needed to push the limit of every boundary I had ever known to excavate my spirit. One way or another I would find a reason to stand on a mountaintop and scream at the top of my lungs, "I am here, and this is who I am!"

2

Thailand

"We travel, some of us forever, to seek other places, other lives, other souls."
—Anais Nin

I felt the unavoidable blast of heat hit me as I exited the airplane upon my arrival in Bangkok. The Land of Smiles greeted me with her warmth in every way possible. I stepped into a new world that felt exotic, frightening, wonderful, strange, and beautiful all at once. At just over 8,000 miles away with about 16 hours of flight time, this was the farthest I had ever traveled from home. Young, naive, and inexperienced in life and love, I had journeyed to Thailand to find myself and to learn what I was capable of. I had come to be bold and push my own boundaries.

Despite the oppressive humidity, I felt wonderfully free and light here, like I could breathe for the first time. Part of me couldn't believe I was in Thailand. Awe and excitement filled me so intensely, it felt as though my heart would burst from my chest. I instantly felt that I was always meant to find this place.

Soon I would see Win. Delirious with anticipation and lack of sleep,

THAILAND

I shot right past baggage claim. Without my luggage, I burst through the exit doors where Win found me. I was too tired to cry, but I melted into his arms. We were reunited after six of the longest months I had ever experienced, full of waiting, with only a letter, an email, or an international phone call sprinkled in between long bouts of silence and longing. That first night in a hotel in Bangkok, Win and I knew each other intimately for the first time.

The next morning, the essences of Thailand saturated all my senses. All around me the sounds of the Thai language rang in my ears like a song. Strong smells that I couldn't identify jolted me into a new dimension. My wide, enchanted eyes flooded under the tsunami of new clothing styles, building architecture, monks dressed in orange robes, and more. At each meal, in proper Thai fashion, my right hand held a spoon, and my left hand a fork. My tongue burned and my mouth puckered from food that was impossibly spicy, sour, and sweet all at once. I instantly loved everything about this place.

Thailand was a break from my life. I was on a semester's hiatus from my university. I had no schedule. I could stop working to meet the rigid standards of the educational system. I was still learning, but now the classroom was life itself.

The school known as Thailand came with its own set of rules which I quickly began to learn. Ironically, rule number one was that an eighteen year old is still a child. It was shortly after Christmas when I went to live with Win's family in a small town in southern Thailand called Betong. Soon, Chinese New Year rolled around. Win's family is Chinese on his father's side and the new year is a hugely celebrated holiday there, regardless of ethnic background. Traditionally, parents, grandparents, aunts, and uncles hand out red envelopes containing money to all the children in their family. As an honorary member of this family, I found myself the recipient of many a red envelope. I wasn't sure how to feel about this. It was sort of wonderful to receive unexpected cash handouts, but back home I had had a job. I had saved up my own money purposefully for this trip. No one my age had a job here. Parents in Thailand financially support their children at least through their university years, if not further.

Rule number two was to respect your elders. In Thailand you always greet people with respect, and that includes understanding your ranking with them. The most obvious thing to distinguish rank is by age. If you are younger, be sure to greet first by placing your hands palms together just in front of your mouth/nose both to say hello and goodbye. This greeting is called "wai." Additionally never point your feet at someone, especially an elder. I was reading a book one evening and lying on my stomach in a room where aunts and uncles were watching TV and chatting. Win quickly swooped in and told me to bend my knees so that my feet would point to the ceiling and not at his aunt at the opposite end of the room.

The third rule was fairly obvious although I didn't fully grasp the gravity of it from the start. Dress modestly. Coming from the United States, I had a different definition of what modest dress meant than the Thai people do. One evening fairly early on, Win's family decided to go out to dinner. I got dressed in a short black skirt, a T-shirt, and a light sweater and pulled my hair into a ponytail. I would feel perfectly comfortable eating outside in this hot, humid place. Only after we returned home, Win, on behalf of his parents, very tactfully suggested that perhaps the next time we went out I might not wear such a short skirt. Being a border town with Malaysia, Betong had quite a thriving prostitution industry. Only after Win connected the dots for me did I see that the only people who wore short skirts were the prostitutes. My American eyes honestly hadn't noticed. In conservative Thailand there's a palpable social stigma against prostitution. It's a bit funny in hindsight, as I can only imagine how Win's family must have felt, publicly treating me to dinner while not saying a word about their discomfort with regard to my attire. After that evening I never wore that skirt again in Thailand.

In this foreign land, it finally made sense for me to feel different. In fact, it finally felt good to feel different. Of course people should stare at my obvious blond hair, pale skin, and round green eyes that so deeply contrasted with their Asian features. In this small city, I was the exotic one. The most hilarious thing was that they treated me like a celebrity. Both of Win's parents were teachers at Betong Wiraratprasan school. Win's mom taught English, so I started going with her most days to the school. I enjoyed feeling useful, helping where I could with the English classes. In the beginning I visited many of the English classes so the students could have an opportunity to meet and speak with a native English speaker. At the end of all those classes you cannot imagine the droves of students who lined up requesting my autograph. Over a few weeks I signed more scraps of paper than I could count. I felt like a star.

Speaking of stars, the blockbuster movie Titanic, which had been released in 1997 was still the topic of a lot of conversation in Thailand. Celine Dion's song "My Heart Will Go On" was on everyone's heart. I'm not sure how it started, but every English class requested that I sing it. I have some singing and voice training background and I knew the song. The concrete classroom walls provided perfect acoustics. During these mini classroom concerts I felt like a real pop star on stage.

I fell into a comfortable routine going to school most days and helping in the classrooms or with correcting homework. I also was handed a job teaching English to adults one evening per week. Win's mom started teaching me some basic Thai. I learned the Thai alphabet and numbers. I got to be able to speak small amounts and perhaps read at a kindergarten level. On weekends Win would take me to spend time with his friends. He had a good core group of friends with whom he had grown up. I enjoyed their company even if I couldn't communicate with them much. Other times some of the students from school would invite me to go get ice cream or go shopping with them. I loved this time. It was simple. It was fun. I was taking it all in.

Win and I really enjoyed being together. We both loved working out so we started going to the free gym one evening a week. On our way home, if it wasn't pouring rain, we would almost always stop and get a quick treat like bananas or corn in coconut milk.

At one point Win insisted on teaching me how to ride a motorbike, although I was terrified and didn't want to learn. It felt like way too much coordination to navigate through traffic, shift gears properly, and stay on the left side of the road. After a few lessons in the parking lot of the pagoda, Win informed me that I would be driving him home. He sat on the back and helped me navigate so I didn't get lost. The quiet streets were easy. The busy intersection was manageable. The last stretch was a steep hill. I was so worried about shifting gears to make it all the way up the hill that I ended up with my wrist awkwardly pulled all the way back on the handle, holding on for dear life the whole way up and into the driveway. Win teased me later as we laughed about my white-knuckled ride home. From then on I always got to be a happy passenger on the back.

Our favorite thing was traveling. We were maybe a 20 minute drive to the border with Malaysia. Just beyond the border was a duty free store. Occasionally Win's family would make a plan to drive down there and shop. It was fun to browse through the various treats available and choose a few to take home. One Saturday Win and I went with a big group of his friends across the border to Malaysia. There were some waterfalls nearby where we spent the day swimming in and exploring the pools. Since we lived so close to the border, that was how I managed to stay in Thailand for six months. Every couple of months someone would drive me to the border crossing. There was a small booth where an attendant checked passports. I would stamp out, ride around to the other side, and stamp back into the country. On paper, I have visited

Malaysia over a half dozen times.

Schools in Thailand are off in April, so the whole family spent a month with Win's mother's relatives in Pang Nga. The famous island of Phuket is just offshore of Pang Nga connected by a bridge. I was excited the first time someone took us for a day trip to one of the beautiful beaches of Phuket. The Andaman Sea was clear blue, warm, and inviting. The salt water stung my eyes as Win's younger cousins splashed gleefully and carelessly chest-deep in the ocean.

On the mainland there was a very unique temple built inside a cave hidden within a mountain. The cave guarded and protected this holy site from weather and from animals, but not tourists. They came in droves. The monkeys that lived on the top of the mountain knew this and ventured down daily to be fed treats. Win and I started coming here many afternoons. We would just sit and watch bus loads of tourists arrive and interact with the monkeys. We got endless pleasure out of this because, for some reason, people expect monkeys to behave as though they're civilized. When a tourist would try to offer a monkey one chip, the monkey would grab the entire bag and run off with it. If a monkey knew that a human had more than one banana, it would threaten the human by snarling and advancing until the poor person flung the banana at the monkey in terror and fled. We couldn't help but laugh at the comedy before us. As there wasn't much else to do in languid, peaceful Pang Nga, this became the highlight of our days.

Songkran, or Thai New Year, also takes place in April. During this holiday people douse each other with water in the streets. Win told me about this custom ahead of time. Many of Win's aunts and uncles who didn't want to get wet would stay in their homes for several days. Win wanted to participate and show me the fun of it. One of Win's uncles who owned a pickup truck loaded up the bed with tubs full of water and plastic containers to use as scoops. Several cousins, friends, Win, and I crammed ourselves in the back among the water vessels armed with our scoops. We drove into town which was a virtual parade of vehicle after vehicle loaded to the brim with water and people. Throngs of people also stood in the streets and pressed all around the vehicles. The scene was pure euphoric mayhem. Drench and be drenched. Squeal, laugh, and celebrate. I furiously got to work scooping water and flinging it on every stranger I saw. I was soaked to the bone before I had time to think. The slow line of cars wound through the town. We could go no quicker than the vehicle in front of us. Inevitably we ran out of water, but we continued to be drenched by everyone who passed us by. I had not known it was possible to be cold in such a hot country, but this was a time I now found myself shivering in the middle of the day with my long, wet hair clinging to my face and my cold soaked clothing plastered to my body. By the time we returned home, I felt like a drowned cat. All I wanted was to feel warm and dry again.

This time in Pang Nga was relaxing, peaceful, and somewhat monotonous. It was here that I started to notice that something was missing. My monthly cycle was late, and as more days went by I started to wonder if that meant what I thought it meant. Win and I figured that our best bet for seeing a doctor privately was to visit a hospital on Phuket. We rode a bus for a "day trip" to the island. Win inquired and found a hospital where I could take a pregnancy test. A doctor entered the room and confirmed that I was pregnant. In his very kind and friendly manner he estimated my due date to be December 16th of the same year 1999. He joked that it would not be a millennium baby. He also gave us the names of two doctors in Hat Yai and Yala, large cities in the south of Thailand, who could "help" us if we decided that we didn't want the baby.

Leaving the hospital I felt dazed. I have never experienced such an extreme mix of contradictory emotions swirling around together inside me. I felt pure elation at the thought of being a mother and I simultaneously felt sheer terror at the thought of telling anyone my news. Win felt similarly. We both wanted children. We just didn't want them yet. That afternoon we talked about having a baby and the conversation was happy. We both still felt shocked by the news, but under the shock on the surface bubbled a warm wave of love for our child. We also discussed the alternative. Win felt like it would be best if we didn't have the baby, but he didn't push the issue. As we rode home that afternoon on the bus we pondered our situation as we browsed the pregnancy brochures we had received from the hospital.

One night a week later several of us sat on the living room floor eating dinner and casually watching TV. Out of nowhere I knew I had to throw up even though I didn't feel sick. I quickly excused myself to the bathroom and immediately threw up my dinner. I crept back and whispered to Win what had happened.

From that point on everything changed. My previously healthy appetite vanished. All food and smells of food made me feel sick. I could keep nothing down. The worst food was a particular fried egg "kai dow," which had previously been my favorite. Everyone knew egg was my favorite and continued to offer it to me every time it was available. When someone would put a bit of egg on my plate, Win would quickly and sneakily snatch it off and eat it himself. It took many years after that for me to be able to look at an omelet or fried egg again without a wave of nausea washing over me.

How I managed to hide my illness from everyone is a mystery. Win and I made ourselves as scarce as possible and found ways to "eat out" instead of spending mealtimes with the family. At the end of April we drove back down south to Betong. A long stretch of the way between Pang Nga and Betong is nothing but a two lane twisty mountain road. It didn't seem so strange to anyone when I became carsick and they had to pull over the car for me to recover.

Back in Betong, Win and I still worked to hide my pregnancy and my now constant nausea. I constantly felt sick and I threw up easily.

We knew we couldn't hide my pregnancy for long so we started having more serious conversations about what we should do. We both felt completely conflicted.

Some days I woke up saying, "Let's have the baby," and we talked about how cute it would be and guessed who it would most resemble. I started having dreams about the baby being born. They were always happy dreams. The first time I dreamed about having the baby she was a girl. The second time, I dreamed he was a boy. We even talked about names we liked. Our baby would have both a Thai and an English name.

Other days Win and I thought about the practicality of having a baby. I would be going back to school and he would soon be entering university. I would be living in the U.S. and he would be living in Thailand. How could we possibly make this work? Those days we came to the conclusion that an abortion would be our best choice.

The pendulum swung back and forth. Having a baby sounded like a happy fantasy. Not having a baby sounded like a practical reality. From day to day we would change our minds. We never came to a firm decision either way. We both really wanted to have the baby, but Win started to voice his belief that it made more sense to have an abortion. Feeling incapable of making my own decision, I started to listen to Win.

It was now well into the month of May, and I became more concerned by the fact that we were allowing so much time to go by than by the actual fact of being pregnant. I was constantly ill, I had dropped 10 pounds, and my emotions lay in tatters all around me as the hormones of pregnancy worked their magic. I was in no position to make the decision I was trying to make, but an emotional rage overtook me one morning as I woke up.

I pleaded with Win, "If we're going to have the abortion then let's just do it." He said he needed to find the right time and the right reason to tell his parents that we wanted to make a trip to Hat Yai. I exploded at him, "You're not the one who's pregnant!" He instantly bolted out of the room and found his parents. He made up a story about me wanting to visit Hat Yai and do some shopping in a big city before I had to leave Thailand. We left by bus the next day. By this time I knew always to carry plastic bags with me so that I could use them whenever I got sick. That long, twisty road was no friend to a pregnant woman, and I used a couple of the bags. I was grateful when we reached our destination and I could sit outside in the fresh air while Win called a friend who lived in Hat Yai.

Win's friend Oh was a former classmate. Oh already had large eyes which nearly bulged out of their sockets when Win told him that I was pregnant. He agreed to help us locate the doctors whose names we had been given that day at the hospital in Phuket. The first doctor they called wouldn't or couldn't perform an abortion. The second doctor was available for such services. We got the address and the clinic hours and headed there late that afternoon.

3

The Darkest Night Of My Soul

> "New beginnings are often disguised as painful endings."
> — Lao Tzu

The date was May 19, 1999. It was Win's 19th birthday. He took me to the clinic. Had he not accompanied me, I believe I would have turned around and walked out. I knew Win wouldn't have forced me to go through with the abortion, but somehow I didn't feel like I had the right to refuse. Knowing that I could have made a different decision and had my baby has been the deepest regret of my life. My final memories of that 10 week pregnancy are of vomiting one final time and seeing the tiny fetus and its heartbeat on an ultrasound.

They led me to a small upstairs room above the clinic. The room was plain and white with no windows. The doctor couldn't take any chances that anyone might see. There I lay down on a makeshift operating table. How could I be about to go through with this? I wouldn't allow myself to think about it. I made myself go numb.

"Sin," the doctor had written on a paper downstairs. His judgment compounded the judgment I had already heaped on myself, and the word stabbed me like a knife in the heart. He also wrote "illegal."

THE DARKEST NIGHT OF MY SOUL

Abortion is illegal in Thailand. The doctor spoke to me in English. He warned me that I could not cry and that when I left I could not speak of this to anyone. He punctuated this by saying, "I don't have to trust you, but you have to trust me." The cold words felt as though they physically punched me in the gut. They sounded ominous and mean. It was as if the doctor himself felt he needed to wash his hands of the matter so his own conscience could somehow be clear. Those words were my final warning.

A middle-aged woman aided the procedure. She mercifully gave me what comfort she could. The woman put a piece of plastic underneath me and gently placed a cloth over my eyes. She politely asked if I spoke Thai. When I answered that I did speak some Thai she asked how long I had been in Thailand and told me she planned to visit California soon. Then I heard the doctor enter the room.

I was given no anesthetic, but the woman held my hand the entire time. I squeezed her hand to prevent myself from crying out. The pain was excruciating. I know now that it was far more painful than natural childbirth. I squeezed the woman's hand desperately as waves of convulsions wracked my body. Less than an hour prior, I had experienced my first ultrasound and seen my baby's heart beating for the first and only time before it was violently ripped from my body. The relentless hum of the machine that vacuumed life out of my uterus still echoes in my ears.

After the procedure, the woman escorted me to another, smaller, dark room where I was to lie down on the bed until I could walk downstairs. I have no idea how I walked there on my own legs. I only remember lying shaking and quivering on the bed. As I writhed in pain from the violence that had taken place inside me, my fingers desperately kneaded the pillow in an attempt to decrease the intensity of the physical suffering I was experiencing. Wave after wave of seemingly endless pain swept through me as my body shivered and shuddered in a tide of agony. These convulsions lasted so long, I didn't believe I could ever stand again.

The worst of the physical pain passed in perhaps 20 minutes. I finally became able to sit, and after another long while to stand. I have only vague shadows of memories from the rest of the day. I slightly remember walking down the stairs. I have one brief snapshot of a memory of being able to eat all my dinner, where previously all food had made me sick. Many times I broke down crying inconsolably. All other memories from that day and the following days are locked up tightly in a vault that my own subconscious keeps from me so that I can carry on.

4

Consequences

"Not the world, not what's outside of us, but what we hold inside traps us."
—Gabor Maté

About a month after the abortion, my six months in Thailand came to an end and I boarded my flight home to the U.S. (Win and I would continue to date long distance for another two years with me spending my school holidays in Thailand.) As planned, I entered a Japanese summer intensive language course at the Middlebury Institute of International Studies at Monterey in California. The fast pace and intense nature of the program was a welcome distraction from the otherwise constant, gut-wrenching grief I was experiencing. The course also disguised the true nature of my distress and made it appear to be stress—the product of a serious student throwing her whole heart and soul into her studies. When my grandfather passed away that summer it was a strangely wonderful and welcome opportunity to be openly sad for a while.

Every day for months my head replayed the most awful loop. I relived the abortion. I asked myself how I could have done it. I imagined

I had chosen a different outcome ... except I hadn't ... so I relived the abortion and questioned my decision and imagined I had chosen differently ... over and over.... I was making myself crazy.

What made me turn to abortion that day? Nothing in my life ever even remotely suggested that abortion was an option for me. I wasn't born an "abortionist." In fact, in accordance with my Catholic faith and education, I had always *known* I would never do such a thing.

I remember in high school having "what if" conversations with my girlfriends. Someone would ask,

"What would you do if you ever got pregnant?"

"I'd have the baby," I would answer confidently.

Only through fear could I have made a decision akin to tearing my own heart out of my body. If only I had understood even an inkling of the damage I would cause myself, I never could have gone through with it. My most immediate symptoms expressed as insomnia, chronic upper back pain, and crying myself to sleep every night. The insomnia eventually went away when I became too tired not to sleep. I learned to manage my stress-induced back pain with exercise. The feelings that forced the floods of tears, however, proved impossible to turn off. Somehow, in the name of survival, I managed to bury those feelings and with them a huge part of what makes me human. It turns out that feelings are an all or nothing package. I tried desperately to ignore the pain and only focus on happy things. The only thing I achieved was dulling all my emotions, so that even when I was genuinely happy I felt only the embers of joy. It would cost me two decades of suffering without knowing the "cure" before I would finally start to find true healing.

In every cell of my body I had wanted to keep my baby. Some people know exactly what they want to be when they grow up. All I ever knew was that I wanted to be a mom, and yet somehow I had allowed fear to take over me that day. I had been a stranger in a foreign country with no support network of family or close friends nearby. My upbringing taught me that people should not have babies outside of marriage. In Thailand, as well, it is extremely rare for people to have children outside of marriage. Win thought that abortion was the best option. I didn't have enough faith in myself to fight for the baby I wanted or to face the unknown world of being a young, unwed mother. I felt utterly unworthy of having this baby.

Now that I had done the unthinkable, my primary goal in life became running so far away from the pain that it could never hurt me again. I tried to hide from it by maintaining an active social life. I tried to outrun it by keeping so busy that it couldn't catch up. I wanted to stop feeling sad. That's all I cared about. What was done was done. I couldn't change the past, I rationalized, and I had to live my own life to the best of my ability. I tried to be stronger than the pain, but there is no such thing.

I thought the only way to live well was to stop being sad all the time. I needed to "get a grip" and manage my emotions so they couldn't manage me. The only problem with this method is that you constantly have to out-maneuver the pain so that you can stay two steps ahead. If you stop to think, the pain will pounce on you unawares. It is completely unsustainable and unrealistic to live this way. I didn't find out until much later that when it comes to emotions, the only way around is through. I had no concept that facing the very thing that was causing me so much heartache is actually the way to clear it.

I finally decided it would be best to tell my mom about the abortion nearly a year after it happened. I didn't feel comfortable telling her, but the constant pain I felt was unbearable. Anything had to be better than keeping that secret. I was home for spring break. My dad was out of town so I slept in my mom's bed with her. One night at bed time I forced myself to spill my story.

I tensely whispered, "Mom, I have to tell you something." I instantly started getting choked up and had to make a hard pause after every few words to swallow. "Um ... When I was in Thailand ... um ... I um ... I got ... pregnant ... and I had ... an abortion."

My mom burst into tears. She hugged me as we both cried.

"How far along were you?" Mom asked through her tears.

"Ten weeks," I sobbed.

Mom finally asked me if she should tell Dad. "No. Please don't tell Dad," I whispered. She wondered if it would be okay to tell her best friend who is also my godmother. "Yes, that's fine," I said.

I knew Mom felt the same need as I did not to hold such heavy news inside her. Of course she should have an outlet for the pain I had just dumped on her. I myself felt a small weight lift off my chest for having shared my dark secret, but I didn't feel better overall, especially having just witnessed my mom break down and cry. She clearly didn't know what to do either. Telling my mom was just scratching the surface of all the layers of the healing work that actually lay ahead of me.

The next ten years were both excruciating and amazing. I charged on with my life because I had to keep going, and I experienced some truly wonderful things. I became an exchange student in Japan in 2000. I made some lifelong friends and amazing memories during my year in Tokyo. In 2002 I graduated from the Middlebury Institute of International Studies at Monterey with a degree in international studies. I worked at the Monterey Sports Center where I first became acquainted with the exercise system known as Pilates. During this same period I met and married someone who shared my passion for all things Japanese. Together we went to Japan on the JET Program from August of 2003 to August of 2006 to teach English in the city of Fukuoka. He knew about the abortion and never judged me for it. He was a kind, gentle person, and we had fun exploring Japan together. Unfortunately, he did not share my desire to have children. Early in our relationship when I didn't want children *yet*, I failed to understand that he didn't want children *ever*. Life felt completely unfair when this realization set in. I started to believe that I was never going to be allowed to have a baby. After we returned to the U.S. we got divorced and went our separate ways. I pursued a Pilates certification. I passed my final practical exam on my birthday, May 28th, in 2008.

While I loved the life I was living, interwoven with all my amazing experiences were always grief, pain, and mourning. I'm deeply grateful for the privileged life I have lived, but for me nothing has ever made up for the loss of my baby. No matter how much time got between me and the abortion, there it still was.

During all this time I came up with no new ideas about what to do to feel better, but for better or for worse, life won't let you forget that you have unfinished business to attend. It will send wake up calls in the form of inconvenience, emotional triggers, self-sabotage, illness, or whatever else it can summon to try to get your attention. That's exactly what happened to me.

For ten years I experienced extreme jealousy along with physical discomfort every time I saw a young mother with her baby. I felt devastated and angry any time I would learn that a friend or relative was pregnant. I sometimes even wished that someone's baby would die. I irrationally felt that if I couldn't have my baby, then no one else should have a baby. Jealousy was eating me alive and I hated how it felt. I tried to ignore it by looking the other way. The Universe responded by ramping-up its signals until finally it started "screaming" at me. I still didn't recognize what was going on for quite some time, but the Universe was desperately trying to get my attention.

Late to the Gate

I already mentioned that my first symptoms after the abortion were back pain and insomnia. Maybe feeling poorly wasn't so bad. I mean, I deserved it, right? At least I'm not hurting someone else. Would you like to know what could be worse than repeated physical discomfort? Missing your best friend's wedding. That's what.

Yes, I missed my best friend's wedding. I was supposed to be one of two bridesmaids. I felt like the worst person in the world.

In 2008 I was living in Dallas where I was completing my Pilates apprenticeship for my certification. My dearest childhood friend Shannon was about to get married. She and her fiance planned to elope accompanied only by their wedding party. My heart soared when Shannon asked me to be a bridesmaid. Then my heart dropped to the pit of my stomach when I heard the wedding would take place in Thailand. I dearly love Thailand and I have hundreds of happy memories of the people I knew, the places I visited, and most of the experiences I had.... But I still had one heavy, heart-breaking, painfully dark memory from my time in Thailand that I carried with me like a boulder. The wedding was to take place in Phuket, where I had first learned that I was pregnant.

I had to work hard to get myself together emotionally. "Come on. You can do this," I coached myself. "This is for Shannon. This is not about you," I reminded myself. "It may be healing to be back there," I tried convincing myself. The knot in my stomach did not go away, and I stuffed it down deeper with all the painful emotions trapped inside me.

I went through the motions and made preparations for my trip. I bought my plane ticket to Thailand. I received my bridesmaid dress and had it altered. I arranged for the time off. A friend offered to drive me to the airport.

CONSEQUENCES

On the day of my departure I was packed and ready to go. I was excited. It had been half a dozen years since I had last visited Thailand. The plan was to leave much earlier than necessary and go to dinner with the friend who was driving me to the airport. We would have plenty of time to eat, chat, and leisurely make our way to the airport.

We had so much time to spare that the plan backfired on us. After checking the clock multiple times and not needing to leave yet, I allowed myself to relax. I relaxed for too long. All of a sudden I checked the clock again and ... we were late! We scrambled to pay the bill and hurried to the car. We raced to the airport and pulled up to check in at the curb. The attendant there told me that I was too late to check in for my flight.

I was stunned. I had flown internationally on many, many occasions and never missed a flight or even come close to being late. There had to be another way. Perhaps there was a later flight. No luck. All flights with this airline were fully booked for the next several days. Maybe I could buy a ticket on another airline and get this one refunded. Grasping at my last straw, I decided to fly to Los Angeles, hoping against hope that I could catch a flight from there that was headed in the right direction.

Upon landing at LAX, I bolted to the nearest ticket counter. I checked with the other airlines to find out who had room on a flight. There was availability, but it would cost about two thousand dollars more than I had paid for my original ticket. I couldn't afford it. I felt absolutely sick.

I emailed Shannon to tell her that I would not be attending her wedding. She was able to receive my email during her stopover in Taipei. Shannon emailed back to say that it was okay. I knew she was sad but that the sadness was numbed from jet lag and the pure exhaustion of traveling such a long distance. I also knew that she forgave me, but it was much harder to forgive myself for feeling that I had let her down.

It was getting late and the airport was beginning to shut down. There were now no more flights back to Dallas. I was stranded in L.A. for the night. I felt so broken that it didn't cross my mind to call a friend who lived in the area. I didn't even get a hotel room. I wanted to be on the earliest flight possible back to DFW, so I decided to sleep in the airport.

I should have gone to a hotel. The airport was quite cold, and I had packed lightly with a tropical climate in mind. I couldn't get comfortable stretched out on a cold bench. Sitting at a table with my head resting on my hands was no better. I was too cold and too uncomfortable to sleep more than 20 minutes here and there. I searched the lonely halls. Not even a convenience store or coffee shop was open through the night.

The next morning I boarded a flight back home. I called my family and a few others to let them know that I was still in the States and why. I felt ashamed and worthless. It was one more thing that I wanted to forget had ever happened. Back in Dallas I took one more day off to get my head straight. I spent that day with a friend at the Fort Worth Zoo. The following day I jumped back into life like nothing had happened.

The Call

The year 2008 rolled on. Though it still haunted me, the abortion nearly a decade ago seemed far away. I got through each abortion anniversary and due date anniversary and did my best not to think about it any other time of the year. The memory dimmed a bit and the pain softened slightly. I felt like I was succeeding in conquering the trauma of the abortion. Then, as life has a way of doing, it gave me a wake up call in the form of a literal phone call.

I was a newly certified Romana's Pilates® instructor working full time at a local Pilates studio in Tucson, Arizona. I lived with two friends in a townhouse where I rented a room. I love Tucson. It is a place where my soul feels at ease. From the moment I first drove into that city I knew without a doubt that I could live there. Something about the unexpected green of the Sonoran desert and the grand backdrop of the Santa Catalina mountains grounded and comforted me. I was living in my dream city and I had my dream job. I made lots of good friends there. I loved my life in Tucson.

Everything was so perfect that I could have fooled myself for the rest of my life into thinking that I was fine. If a negative emotion or a hint of remorse washed over me I could always work out rigorously at the studio or go on a great hike to re-bury my heart and clear my mind again. It was too easy to hide from my past in the peace of the desert.

One lovely day in September, I got a call from Tahera, one of my best friends from college. She was a single mother with three children and had just learned that she was about to have a fourth. Tahera decided she was going to have an abortion this time rather than go through the tireless, thankless work of parenting an infant by herself again with three other children in tow. She wanted to know what to expect so she could get ready for it.

This call out of the blue was like a punch in my gut. Tahera was one of the first people whom I had told about the abortion when I still didn't feel like I could tell anyone. Ironically, at the time Tahera judged me for my decision (although she was mature enough to keep her judgment mostly to herself.)

I felt deeply for Tahera and I grieved for myself and my own unborn baby. Why was this coming up again? I'm not even sure I was able to give Tahera the best advice. She was living in California where abortion was legal, whereas I had gotten an illegal abortion. She would have access to a certain standard of care that had not been available to me. For the first time it struck me how little I knew about an abortion procedure in spite of having had one myself. No one who was well-informed helped me weigh the options. No one told me how the procedure worked. No one explained what I could expect during or after the procedure. No one reassured me that I could still have children in the future. I never got so much as a pamphlet. I felt unqualified to tell Tahera anything, but I did my best to share my experience.

Tahera asked about the procedure itself. "Will it hurt?" she asked, and "What exactly will they do?" My only memories were of excruciating pain, as I was given no anesthetic. Tahera would, of course, not feel any pain during the procedure itself. She might feel some pain after the anesthesia wore off. I described how the body would return to a natural cycle again, similar to how the body returns to fertility after pregnancy. I also told her that she might produce a small amount of breast milk after the abortion, though not a lot, and it would probably dry up quickly.

Of course Tahera also wanted to know how she would feel emotionally. This might have been the hardest question for me to answer. What was the best adjective? Wrecked? Devastated? Torn apart? As much as I hated to admit it, I was still feeling all those things. In fact, they were bubbling up inside me as we spoke. I did my best to stay calm, compassionate, and in control while on the call, but as soon as we hung up I knew I was not okay.

I was supposed to attend a football game at the University of Arizona that evening with some friends. We were in line waiting to buy tickets and I started to feel like I couldn't hold myself together. I was going to cry. I would never make it through the game, let alone enjoy it. I apologized to my friends and excused myself to return home.

That evening I started researching abortion recovery and counseling services online.

5

Good Grief

"Grief can be the garden of compassion. If you keep your heart open through everything, your pain can become your greatest ally in your life's search for love and wisdom."
—Rumi

Emotional healing is tricky because emotions are elusive and abstract. They're not concrete and visible like a cut to the skin. Where is an emotion and how can you possibly control or change it? The key to reaching an emotion is to go straight to your body's operations control center—the brain. That's the place which sends the messages to create new skin cells when a cut occurs. That same brain demands the production of certain chemicals within our body that directly affect the way we feel. The way to heal emotionally, therefore, is to rewire the brain.

Why wasn't my brain wired properly in the first place? It actually was. At least it was until new circumstances came into my experience. I never had an abortion until I did, so my former brain never had to be wired to process such an event or have a plan in place for my healing if said event occurred. Why not? It's because that would have taken energy—*lots* of it. Why would my body spend its energy predicting my worst-case scenario and designing a search-and-rescue mission for a fantasy event? That would deplete my resources that I was relying on to stay alive and function at a high level. Tragically, I made a decision that went against all the moral coding I had ever assembled in my former brain. My brain did not have the circuitry in place to handle this, and the motherboard exploded.

System update please! For optimal use of modern technology, we frequently update the operating systems. Our brains require exactly the same optimization. Unfortunately, we can't just plug our head into some device to receive the required download. Also there's no handbook telling us what specific new wiring we need or how to acquire it. That's why it took me many years of trial, error, despair, and prayer to find something that helped me. The good news is that our brains can be rewired. The bad news is that, while it is essentially simple, it is not necessarily quick.

Our brains are powerful! If we think a thing is so, then we are right. If I believe I'm emotionally injured from an abortion I'll find all the supporting evidence to prove myself correct. I spent twenty years doing that. In case you're wondering, I was always right.

As powerful as our brains are, they are equally malleable. If I believe I'm healed after an abortion I'll produce equally strong evidence to support my case. How can that be? I'm genuinely still sad because I don't have my baby. I can't turn back time and make a different decision. Nothing changes, so nothing is healed, right? Fortunately it turns out that I have the power to change my thinking *in spite of my circumstances*!

I've shared my journey into the heart of pain with you. Now please allow me to describe the steps I took to find my way back to peace. I had no counsel and not the faintest clue where to start, but I was determined to figure it out.

When I decided once and for all to heal from abortion, the first thing

I learned was how to grieve. Earlier, when I allowed my sad thoughts to remain on an endless loop, I was not grieving. That was a form of self-torture. Grieving is un-negotiable when healing from the trauma of abortion. Whether the loss happened yesterday or 70 years ago, mourning begins the moment you give yourself permission to be sad. For too long, I fell into the trap of thinking that I didn't deserve to feel sad for something I had done. I'm here today to say that we all have a right to every single feeling that comes up inside of us no matter the cause. The truth in the case of abortion is that a potential human being ceases to exist. There were never any guarantees that my pregnancy would result in the birth of a living baby, but nonetheless, I felt the same as if someone had died. I get to feel sad about that.

What do people normally do when someone dies? We cry. We gather with friends and share memories. We attend funeral services. We visit a grave or memorial site. We do things to honor a life so that we can create closure around the fact that this person is no longer with us in the flesh.

The baby that was forming inside me was real, but that being is no longer physically here. The pain of that loss was and is real for me. For this reason, I had an obligation to myself to do things that helped me create closure. No one ever has to feel okay about any painful past decision, but we all still have beautiful lives to live. No human can truly thrive in the shadows of suppressed emotions around trauma. An emotion held hostage becomes toxic to the body that holds it. I had way too much life still ahead of me. I wasn't going to risk being depressed or sick for the rest of my life.

I had no healing checklist when I set out to mend my emotional wounds, but I can see that I went through a clear and specific process. Basically, there were five steps to my healing. First, I allowed myself to mourn the loss of my child. Not grieving was like telling a river not to flow. The dam was going to burst one day no matter how well

I reinforced those walls. Second, I found support in such places as counseling, groups, and retreats. There's a lot we can do by ourselves, but healing should not be a solo activity. It always works best when loving hearts and helping hands come together. Third, I opened myself up to infinite possibility. I felt like I had tried everything to heal and nothing was working, but I refused to believe that there was no hope for my healing. I leaned into faith and discovered that miracles are eager to show up for us when we create the right conditions to allow them to flow into our lives. Fourth, I remembered that I'm amazing. I had forgotten or stopped believing this somewhere along the way. When I mentally scanned through my life, a powerful memory resurfaced that reminded me beyond a shadow of a doubt that I am a great human and a wonderful mother. Finally, I learned to tell a new story. I couldn't change the details of the past, but I could stop living the sad story. In fact, I learned that I could re-know the past simply by changing my lens.

Listed out, the five steps are as follows:

5 Steps to Healing

1. Grieve
2. Find Support
3. Open Yourself to All Possibility
4. Re-Know Yourself (Remember All the Ways You're Amazing)
5. Tell A New Story (Stop Living in the Sad Story)

The steps don't have to be taken in any particular order. You can start anywhere and jump back and forth with where you focus your efforts. Some of the steps may be combined. For example, I started my grieving process in tandem with seeking support. The most important thing to keep in mind is that whatever you may feel around abortion is an emotion. To heal around a strong emotion you must allow yourself to feel it, even if feeling it seems like an awful experience. Grieving is the natural way to allow sadness to flow out of you, so the sooner you can grieve the sooner you will find peace. The second most important thing is not to try to release all the pain, grief, anger, etc. all at once. That actually will not feel okay to a body that has become accustomed to holding pain. Expect and allow it to release drip by drip over as long a period of time as it takes.

It is said that Love brings up all that which is unlike itself to be healed. Therefore thank you Guilt and Grief. Thank you Shame and Worthlessness. Thank you Doubt and Judgment. You have served me in the best ways that you knew how. Now it is time for you to go. In the name of Love I command you to leave.

6

Support

"It is support that sustains us on the journey we've started."
—Marci Shimoff

Healing is not a solo journey. You were never meant to walk this path alone, nor will you gain any benefit for attempting to do so. When you're ready you must reach out and begin to choose your support network.

Individual Counseling

I felt hurt and a bit put out when I didn't easily and quickly find much information online for where to go for grief or emotional counseling after an abortion. There was very little that came up, no matter what wording I used for my search. Fortunately for me, I did come across a few things that looked promising. The city of Tucson had several crisis pregnancy centers and it looked like they might offer some type of care or counseling, so that was where I started. It turned out that one of these crisis pregnancy centers in particular was a gem of a place for someone like me to go.

SUPPORT

Making that phone call was the worst. I had spent ages trying not to talk about the abortion or even remember it. It felt like my throat locked up when I actually did want to talk about it. I cannot even remember what words I choked out when the receptionist answered the phone. Somehow I managed to inquire about their post abortion care services. They did offer counseling. Thank God! It was free? Hallelujah! I made an appointment to go in the very next week.

I was terrified walking into that office. I felt like the receptionist and everyone waiting must see right through me and know exactly why I was there. The waiting area was comfortable but I barely noticed. Filling out paperwork was excruciating, as it took me on a 60 second fast-forwarded journey through the worst moments of my past. Okay, that was done. The tears were mostly in check. Now I just had to sit until they called me back. I may have just sat there. I may have idly flipped through a magazine. I honestly don't remember anything but the terror and extreme discomfort I felt at finally facing my fears.

Kathy came out to greet me. She was so calm and gentle in manner that I instantly felt at ease and knew I could trust her. She led me to a room with a small sofa where I could sit and spill out my heart all over the place. Kathy prompted me kindly to share my abortion story and responded with such great empathy that I felt as close to being at ease as I possibly could. She was a Christian counselor and had experienced an abortion herself. Kathy was like an angel from heaven sent to wrap me in a blanket of loving support. She taught me two very important things that day. First, I was allowed to grieve for my child. Second, I was allowed to forgive myself. Kathy quoted Psalms 103:12 to remind me repeatedly that God forgives everyone, no matter what. "As far as the east is from the west, so far has He removed our transgressions from us." She reminded me as many times as I required that love is only and always unconditional. All these years I had damned and condemned myself ruthlessly. Now here was this stranger showing me nothing but mercy and compassion. Mercy for myself felt instantly right and yet I had a hard time believing it should be so easy. Kathy never faltered or became frustrated with me. She remained steady in her manner the entire time we spoke together. I could see that she was a person who had once walked in my shoes and who had forgiven herself. Kathy met me exactly where I was. I am forever grateful that she was the first person to give me guidance. I had needed that deep love to boost me on the start of my healing path.

I cannot stress enough the benefit of seeking out a good professional counselor. Someone who is trained to guide you in managing your emotional state will both provide comfort as well as give you tools to manage those emotions in healthy and productive ways.

Group Support

In addition to continuing my counseling sessions with Kathy, I joined a group that would meet weekly for eight weeks and follow a Bible-based course called *Forgiven and Set Free* by Linda Cochrane. I was so eager to do anything that would aid and speed up my healing that I jumped at this opportunity. It also connected me to other people who needed healing from abortion. While I don't wish this experience on anyone, it was a relief to know that I wasn't the only one suffering under the same burden. About eight or so of us met every Tuesday. We shared our stories, read scripture, completed written homework assignments, and discussed the process of healing. We even opted to extend our time together by two weeks so that we could spend extra time on some of the material. This simple class was actually the pavement to the path I had started walking. It cleared mental debris and smoothed my emotions while helping me understand the work required to get me where I was going. A bonus to joining the group was that I finally got to start connecting with other women, from all walks of life, who had experienced abortion, and I developed bonds with them. I am still in contact with a friend who I met in that class.

Name Your Child

During the class we had the opportunity to name our child(ren) if we chose. Choosing a name dignifies a soul as having been a human child, and it dignifies the mother or father as being a parent. I named my baby Tatiana because I remembered how much I liked that name when I was eighteen. For the first time I allowed myself to be who I had always wanted to be. I allowed myself to be a mother.

Crafts

One of the therapeutic things they suggested at the center was the possibility of making a memorial quilt square so that many quilt squares could be stitched together into one quilt. While I liked this idea, I felt I had too much healing yet to do to fit into just one square. I decided to learn how to make a quilt. A friend's mother who enjoyed quilting eagerly agreed to teach me how to quilt. I used materials that she had remaining from previous projects. She taught me the basics of putting a quilt together as well as different hand stitching techniques. I also got a bit creative drawing and cutting out shapes that would make up the design.

Making a quilt is not everyone's cup of tea, but it is highly therapeutic. I worked through my sadness for hours on end after work in the evenings and over the weekends. I finally had a productive way to channel all that hurt. The brilliant thing is that I turned pain into something beautiful and useful that represents something important and specific.

The only mistake I made here was in giving myself a condition. "When

I finish this quilt I will be healed," I promised myself. Big mistake. Healing is not something that can be dictated or otherwise controlled. There is no perfect way or time to heal. The quilt itself is far from perfect and would not likely win any prizes. With healing, everything I do in its name is the right thing to do in the moment, and it's actually not my job to decide when and how much I require. I am only to notice how I feel in every moment and discern what is the next right thing to do. To this day my quilt is close to being complete but it remains unfinished.

Retreats

Another place where the center connected me was with Rachel's Vineyard. This is a wonderful program that leads weekend retreats specifically for healing from abortion. I signed up for the next one, which would be offered in October. An entire weekend dedicated to healing is intense, lovely, peaceful, and sad and magnifies every emotion times 100. It also allows you to immerse yourself in the healing process in such a way that no distraction can call you away from the work.

This was a Catholic retreat, which meant a lot to me. I desperately needed the Church to tell me that not only was I forgiven but that I was accepted exactly for who I was, no explanation necessary. There were two priests who participated during that weekend. They offered the kindest words and the warmest hugs I had received in a long time.

Everything in the retreat was full of meaning and the weekend was very well organized. The first thing that stood out to me was that first evening. There were maybe 20 participants, as well as several facilitators, including one man. Seated comfortably in a candle-lit room, we took a long time to go around and allow everyone to share the story of her or his personal abortion experience(s). I remember feeling so sad that evening. It felt like 10 years' worth of grieving was bubbling up from very deep below the surface and saturating every part of my being before flooding the room around me. It felt good finally to let myself feel so sad. In fact, the next day, one of the girls gave me a rosary that she had bought me at the retreat center gift shop. She said I had just looked so sad and she hoped the rosary might offer me some comfort. I still own those rosary beads and I'll treasure them forever as a symbol of kindness and goodwill from one grieving soul to another.

The first afternoon when we resumed after lunch we found various large rocks, all natural and all uniquely different, placed on a large coffee table around which we sat. We were each to choose a rock that somehow called to us. I noticed a large rock that somewhat resembled a heart. It looked hollow in one of its upper chambers. I snagged it. After everyone had chosen a rock, each person got an opportunity to explain why she had chosen that particular one. I explained that mine looked exactly how I felt—like a heart with a huge piece missing, as though it had been ripped out. The next part of the exercise was ongoing and it was eye-opening. The rock represented the suffering that we carried. We were to bring that rock everywhere with us—to the bathroom, to dinner, to the shower, to bed, etc. We had to tend it until we decided to let it go. There was no timeline by which we had to release the rock. If we never gave it up that was okay. I was shocked to feel how difficult it was to put that rock down. I think only one woman gave hers up that very afternoon. It took me more than 24 hours before I decided that I would be okay putting the rock down. I was floored to realize that, as much as I disliked my suffering, I hated the idea of parting with my suffering even more. I learned a lot about human nature that day. The stories we tell ourselves we make real. We attach ourselves to them as though we are our stories. Part of me had even wanted to name that rock as though it was actually my child or my pet. Can you imagine how much harder it would have been to give up my rock if I had personalized it and endeared it to me? Yet I realized that's exactly what I had done with my suffering. Without a baby to hold, I had clung to a nightmare instead. It was a poor substitute for what I actually desired.

To me, the most powerful ceremony we performed during the retreat was the lighting of candles for our children. It was another candle-lit evening. A glass bowl of water sat in the center of the room. Each of us in turn approached the vessel and lit a floating candle and spoke a name for every aborted child. One woman lit seven candles and spoke seven names. The plain bowl of water had become a beautifully radiant beacon. In this moment I could see all these souls. They were not lost! In fact, they were shimmering and peaceful. Their light comforted me with the knowledge that they were not alone. They were all together and their light could never be diminished no matter how many abortions we collectively had. I still cried for my loss, but I slept more peacefully that night picturing Tatiana joyfully playing with her companions.

Visit A Place of Worship

Several weeks later I decided to go to confession one morning before I attended mass. Catholics practice confessing their sins to a priest, and I had never actually confessed the abortion. In fact, I hadn't been to confession in years. Through the tears, I told the priest that I had had an abortion and how sorry I felt. He gave me the most perfect reply. "Let the past be in the past." He was an older priest, a bit gruff, and spoke with an accent, but his words sounded like the bell of freedom tolling. "Let the past be in the past." The words were so simple, wise, and kind. He didn't tell me to forget my experience. He reminded me that I needed to let it be. I was here in this present moment. Why should I be so hung up on something from ten years ago? It was the lesson of the stone all over again. Apparently I needed this lesson multiple times and in a variety of forms.

Embrace Your Mistakes

Healing is nothing like what I imagined it must be. On one hand, I'm never going to "fix" the un-fixable. On the other hand, there was never really anything wrong. I veered off the path. I got lost for a while. Once I realized this, I found my way back. After all, we can only ever start where we are. We can't start where we "should be."

Today I have three children whom I regularly counsel to celebrate their mistakes. "Yay mistake!" I cheer when they get down on themselves for doing something wrong. I don't even like the word "wrong" anymore because it's nothing but a judgment. Doing something "wrong" guides you closer to the way to do it "right." My children tend to feel frustrated when I cheer because they want to stay in their own judgment of themselves and feel upset. I tell them they don't actually have to feel happy to say the words "yay mistake." It's not about changing your feelings. It's about acknowledging that you're one step closer to where you want to be.

I can never erase my painful feelings. I can only change how my mind thinks about an event by choosing a different reaction. The truth is I will always regret having had an abortion. What I will not continue to do, though, is keep judging myself for it.

All I can ever do is take an ugly thing and make it beautiful. Just like with the quilt, it represents something that made me sad for a long time, but I organized it in such a way that when I stand back and look at the whole thing, it's a gorgeous piece of art. It can even keep me warm.

Healing reminds me a lot of gardening. "Weeds" or "bad thoughts" are always going to pop up in the spaces I've cleared. I repeatedly have to clear the weeds over and over again and become mindful about what fills the new empty spaces. It's labor intensive because I didn't just get sad for a day or a week or a month. I stayed sad for twenty years! There is some serious reprogramming required here. It starts with me intentionally noticing my thoughts instead of passively allowing thoughts to float through my brain. When I notice that I'm feeling sad, for example, I can allow myself to feel the sadness while at the same time saying something like, "I made a mistake when I terminated my first pregnancy and I completely accept, love, and forgive myself."

7

The Deepest Longing Of My Heart

"In my deepest, darkest moments, what really got me through was a prayer."
—Iyanla Vanzant

The personal work I did in the fall of 2008 was big and it took me a long way in terms of healing, but it set the stage for a long winter. Earlier I mentioned that intense healing must only happen one drop at a time. In my case it was like even the drips stopped. I had made a good start. I felt much better although I still didn't feel fine. It felt like all healing momentum stopped in its tracks. I was going to have to sit on this plateau of partial healing for another ten years.

Beginning the healing work was very necessary for a couple of reasons. For one thing it started to untie some of the knots where I had experienced emotional blockages. For another, it got some forward momentum going so that I started to feel hopeful instead of stuck. What the work did was allow me to open up to the possibility of having the family I wanted, even though my heart wasn't fully healed yet. It was during this time that I got married to a kind man named Jay whom I told about the abortion and who accepted that I still had healing work to do around it. Together Jay and I have had three children.

I always knew that having children would not make up for my unborn child. Fortunately, if anything, the abortion allowed me to feel that much more appreciation for my living children. Thus, while it has been my greatest joy to be a wife and mother, I still had healing work to do around the abortion. I knew this, but I also felt that I could shift my focus for a while to tend and raise my children.

I had 20 months between the birth of each child. That kept me busy both physically and emotionally. I also got far less than adequate sleep for the better part of four years. My energy reserves were completely drained and I perpetually felt like a zombie—not dead but not quite alive. After the birth of my oldest son I started developing eczema which worsened and worsened over those years until it covered my entire body. I was living my dream of being a mother while wrapped in a nightmare of nutritional deficiencies multiplied by gluten intolerance—only I didn't know any of this yet. I had a lot to learn, quickly, about how to heal on a physical level before I could fully return my attention to my emotional and spiritual healing.

I could write another book on returning to health in my body, but for now I'll keep it short. I bounced back and forth from doctor to doctor who could not stop or reverse my worsening condition. One day a friend randomly introduced me to a chiropractor who also happened to be a nutritionist. She was able to order genetic testing for me and read the results to understand my body's needs. She recommended some dietary changes and a supplement protocol.

Finally, my suffering started to turn around as I began to heal. My skin started to clear. I noticed my energy levels returning. It felt amazing to wake up in the morning with energy to get out of bed! I felt like a new person. This "new person" reveled in the wonder of feeling fine again. I would never again take for granted smooth, clear, comfortable skin or the energy required to get out of bed each morning.

As I got used to feeling well, my attention was freed up to revisit a painfully persistent topic that still needed attention.....

In December of 2018, my child's would-be 19th birthday approached. Even though by now I could make it through her December 16th due date without suffering a meltdown, I still felt like some lost chamber within my heart remained frozen. The coming spring would bring the 20th anniversary of the abortion. Twenty years! How was it possible that after two decades I still hadn't fully learned how to heal?

I felt frustrated that I was still so lost. Even though the years were sprinkled with counselors, recovery groups, retreats, and opening up to family members about the abortion, I felt as though I had plateaued at around 90% recovered. What more was I supposed to do? Why couldn't I just heal?! I wanted to be fully happy again.

My frustration turned into desperation. That month of December in 2018 I started praying a daily prayer. "Please help me release that which does not serve." It was desperate. It was simple. It was honest. It was the most vulnerable and true thing I had ever prayed.

This prayer poured forth from my heart daily. One day I randomly noticed a Facebook ad for a program called Your Year of Miracles lead by Marci Shimoff and Dr. Sue Morter. Intrigued, I signed up for one of the free masterclass information calls they were offering. I immediately resonated with these women and their message of opening to miracles through faith and practical action guided by love. I hadn't worked in several years. I had very little money in my savings account. With my heart in my stomach, I took a deep breath and signed up. Surely my emotional health and freedom were worth the $599 price of admission. Dr. Sue read some of the names of people who had just signed up. When I heard "Elizabeth from Texas," My heart burst into song while I simultaneously quivered in fear. That evening, still feeling both elated and terrified, I shared with Jay the bold move I had made. I was ready for a change. I was ready for miracles. I was ready to open to all possibility.

8

Miracles

"There are only two ways to live your life. One is as though nothing is a miracle. The other is as though everything is a miracle."
—Albert Einstein

The weekend of January 12-13, 2019, Jay and I headed to Austin where we would attend a workshop led by Paul Selig. Paul Selig is, among other things, a medium and author of several channeled texts. Jay and I had been eagerly reading all his books as soon as each was released, so we were very excited to attend a live workshop with the channel himself.

Before going to the workshop I prayed that the Guides would support me in releasing that which did not serve me and which was preventing my healing. I had no idea what to expect and entered the event on Saturday morning full of excitement and curiosity. After a brief introduction of himself, Paul went right into channeling the Guides. During that first channeling session I felt as if the Guides were speaking specifically to me. I heard loud and clear the message that the past choices we made were the perfect and only choices we could have made in the vibration we held. I was floored by this unexpectedly perfect message. I felt like crying with relief.

Mid-morning or so, Paul instructed us to pair up with someone we didn't know and designate a partner "A" and a partner "B." I got paired up with Paul Selig's assistant, Dustin. Right away I noticed something strange. We were instructed to look directly into each other's eyes while speaking, but for some reason, I didn't feel I could maintain eye contact with Dustin. I didn't feel embarrassed or nervous. To this day I cannot explain why I couldn't look into his eyes. Instead I stared at his neck. The other thing that I noticed was how uncomfortable my body felt. We had been sitting for around two hours at this point, so standing up should have felt great. I had eaten a full breakfast, I was hydrated and healthy, and I was wearing comfortable shoes. I noticed no cramps, aches, or pains anywhere in my body, yet somehow, I felt physically uncomfortable. I couldn't put my finger on the source of my discomfort. I clasped my hands behind me to open my chest. Normally this helps me release stress, but it provided zero relief today. I interlaced my fingers in front of me, but that felt worse. I lengthened my arms down my sides and still felt unexplainably uncomfortable. I decided just to focus on the words I was to repeat.

I was partner "A," which meant that I would be the first to repeat Paul's channeled words to my partner. The words we repeated were affirmations of the being standing before us. It was a beautiful way to witness a fellow human being.

Then it was Dustin's turn to repeat exactly the same words to me. As he started speaking, I began to feel nauseous. I quickly started to feel increasingly worse and I became alarmed when I realized that I was about to vomit all over this stranger. No sooner did that thought pass through my brain, then I began feeling dizzy. My peripheral vision started to recede. Everything started to appear foggy and all sound became muffled. I braced myself with my left hand and rested my head against the wall. I faintly heard Dustin asking if I was alright. I think I managed to shake my head no before I blacked out....

I slowly eased back into consciousness several minutes later slumped forward in a chair. Dustin and another woman were watching and tending me. Dustin asked my name and if I remembered where I was. I heard myself answer correctly although the words sounded quiet and muffled and I felt like I was far away from my body.

Someone handed me a bottle of water. As I sipped it I became acutely aware that I was blazing hot. I felt as if steam must be rising off of me. I couldn't peel my jacket off quickly enough. I felt weak and shaky. I had very little strength to stand up, so I remained seated in the back of the room. I wasn't even able to find or contact Jay.

After the partnering activity there was time for comments. People raised their hands to share their experience. I shot my hand up in the air and the microphone was passed to me. I told the group that I had passed out. I briefly shared my experience. Paul was able to channel the Guides who declared that I had asked for this.

The rest of the day I felt extremely weak and tired, as though I had just been deathly ill and today was the first day I was feeling better. I ate lunch at lunch time and participated in the rest of that day's workshop. When we broke for the day I went upstairs to our hotel room and found some hotel stationery and a pen. Dustin had suggested that I might journal about my fainting experience to see what, if anything, came up for me.

My pen needed no guidance. The immediate message that appeared on the page was that I had released a past un-forgiveness of myself.

When I stopped writing, I sat for a moment and recalled the memory of the abortion and was amazed to discover that the strangest transformation had occurred. Where previously I felt despair, grief, fear, isolation, and pain, I now felt comfort, compassion, love, empathy, and peace. The memory didn't change. The image I hold of the event is still emblazoned in my brain, but somehow my perspective shifted. For twenty years, every time I thought of the abortion, I was still inside the body of my 18 year old self looking through terrified eyes at a cold-hearted doctor surrounded by the four walls of a relentlessly sterile room housing a machine of torture and death. Now, by contrast, I'm no longer in my body looking out. Instead I hover above the people in the room. I look down with compassion filling my heart at a girl who does not yet know that she is worthy of everything she desires. I shine gratitude on an angel of an assistant holding the girl's hand, trying to provide what comfort she can. I say a prayer of forgiveness for a conflicted doctor who doesn't know how to stand up for his own convictions.

How can the exact same image conjure up such completely different emotions? My previous feelings are as opposite as night is to day. I honestly feel like someone flipped a switch on inside my brain. The crazy thing is I never even knew that I was bumbling around in darkness all those years. I honestly could not see the infinite other number of perspectives through which I could have viewed my experience. It was like I was watching a movie that was so gripping that I felt as though I was the main character. The problem is that for twenty years I never realized I could turn the movie off or simply look away from the screen at absolutely anything else. I literally had to faint and get out of my own way in order to drop the boulder of sorrow that obscured all vision. In a room full of humans witnessing humans, I surrendered to that collective energy and completed the work I had formerly been unable to accomplish alone.

I will always regret my decision to have an abortion. The difference now is that I no longer allow my past regrets to hold power over me. I am an imperfect person who made a deeply painful and egregious error of judgment, *and* I am worthy of infinite love. Walking in grief and clinging to depression does not allow me to live the life I am capable of living. Furthermore, if I'm denying myself love, regardless of the reason, how can I fully love those around me? The answer is I can't. No one can give better to another than one gives to the self. I choose to love myself and shine that light of love outwardly to the whole world.

In hindsight I have sat in gratitude and said many prayers of thanks because I realize that my prayer "Please help me release that which does not serve" was answered in one fell swoop on that January morning in 2019. Furthermore, gratitude continually sweeps over me in waves when I consider all the things that came together in perfect synchronicity to make that moment possible. First, I was paired with Paul Selig's assistant, someone who worked regularly with the messages from the Guides. Second, as I lost consciousness he prevented me from falling to the ground and injuring myself. Third, there were other participants of the workshop who managed to care for me in a calm manner that assisted my recovery while not disrupting the larger group. Fourth, I received a direct verbal communication from the Guides that I had asked for this, and I knew in my heart that my prayer had been answered. There are so many nuances to this miracle, that every time I notice one I feel awe-struck by the perfection of the Creator and this benevolent Universe that supports me.

9

Infinite Possibility

"Our key to transforming anything lies in our ability to reframe it."
—Marianne Williamson

Learning to recognize miracles allowed me to see miracles where I never expected they could be. In the group Your Year of Miracles (YOM) we were instructed to keep a miracles journal and record anything that we can consider a miracle or a "win." The very first miracle I recorded was of fainting and waking up with a new perspective.

Humans are naturally biased toward seeing the negative, but when we train our minds how to see the positive, then the everyday miracles, big and small, start to become more obvious until they jump out from around every corner. From watching the rabbit munch on grass in the yard, to appreciating money when it flowed my way, to relishing a breeze on a hot summer day, to celebrating synchronicities, I learned how to have little moments of gratitude for it all.

When we stop focusing on the negative, bad things don't go away, but they fall to the background where they don't hold as much power. One day I noticed an unauthorized charge on my debit card and had to call the bank. I still had to endure the anxiety of waiting for the $300 charge to be reversed and the annoyance of not having a debit card while I waited to receive its replacement. With my new frame of mind, however, I easily noticed how helpful the bank employee was who assisted me over the phone. I felt grateful when the new card arrived quickly. I thanked the money for being in my account in the first place. I find it much easier to navigate life's challenging situations while focused on what's right than to navigate those same experiences with a heavy emphasis on what's wrong.

Dr. Sue Morter talks about something called the "Quantum Flip®" both in Your Year of Miracles and in her own work with the Morter Institute. She explains how it's possible for everyone to have this total and instant change in perspective. I understand it like a coin. Take any coin and it has a "heads" side and a "tails" side. If you happen to be looking at the tails side of a U.S. quarter, for example, you might describe that coin as having an eagle with spread wings depicted on it. If, instead, you happen to be holding that same quarter on the heads side, you might instead describe it as bearing George Washington's profile. Either way, you would be correct. It just depends on the perspective of you, the observer.

Sometimes a Quantum Flip® happens in the form of an "aha moment." That's happened to you, right? You happen to receive new information or interpret old information in a new way that suddenly sheds light on a situation or shifts your perspective.

When I fainted I experienced a Quantum Flip®. Somewhere between blacking out and returning to consciousness, I discovered a new lens through which to view the abortion. While the scenario in my memory may not have changed, somehow my thoughts and feelings around how I observe it changed. It's a little bit like watching a violent battle scene in a movie out of focus, but it goes way beyond blurry vision. Somehow, softening my vision also softened my feelings. It didn't dull them, mind you. It actually expanded my feelings and put them in balance.

I had never before given myself any grace, leniency, or forgiveness for choosing abortion. Ever since fainting, however, I can only feel love, empathy, and compassion for my past self. This gift of new sight was a gift of hindsight. I decided that I wanted to write a "hindsight story" so that I could fill in the details. I would make it as vivid as possible and read it over and over. Telling a new story is something that everyone should do when looking to shift perspective. In my case I had already changed my inner lens before writing it, but I could have written this story even before I thought it was true. In fact, I wish I had, and I recommend that everyone write a better story about a disappointing past. You can do it for anything. You don't change any of the known facts. You literally just change how you could interpret the details. It requires you to zoom way out and see all possible perspectives, true or not, and ask yourself what if. What if that doctor who performed the abortion was in desperate financial need at the time and couldn't refuse any income? What if the kind woman who helped the procedure was actually going to take the day off to tend her sick grandchild but at the last minute someone else was available so that she could go to work after all? It's all possible. I don't have to know the exact truth in order to be compassionate, loving, and kind to myself. I can write my alternative story as many times and as many different ways as I please. For this story I have one particular version that resonates with me.

* * *

My Hindsight Story

I am the Angel of Mercy, and I knew they were coming. I saw the couple walk into the clinic that morning in May. The girl was American and the boy was Thai. They had struggled with the decision of what to do ever since they learned that they were going to have a baby. They finally decided to travel to a big city where they had heard there was a doctor who could terminate the pregnancy. They were far enough away from family that no one would ever have to find out. They didn't understand that what they needed most was loving support. That's why I waited for them. If they would enlist no earthly help, I would be there for them and do my best to hold them up from my angelic realm.

I knew that in their hearts neither one wanted to have an abortion, but humans can be quite stubborn. They were both allowing their heads to make decisions of the heart! I tried to give them a final message that would help them change their minds. I showed them the image of their baby through a sonogram. I saw how it grabbed the girl's heart, but she reacted differently than I had hoped. Instead of allowing the love to flow, she erected a wall around her heart.

The doctor was a good man. He took care of babies and children. He often wrestled with his own power to take a life, but he was struggling with debt and didn't see how he could refuse money when it came his way. At the end of the day, he ran a business that provided for his own family. If a client requested and paid for his services, he would reluctantly terminate a pregnancy. For him, this day was another busy day. He couldn't understand me when I told him that the girl needed compassionate guidance.

When the doctor used the word "sin," I saw the girl's heart quiver with pain. She quickly fortified the wall around her heart. When he reminded her that abortion is illegal I felt her go cold. Out of the doctor's own fear, he told the girl that while he didn't have to trust her, she had to trust him. In that instant I watched the girl withdraw completely.

As a being of Mercy, my gift is that of loving vision. I can see people only as perfect, though they may judge themselves harshly and walk a precarious path. I forgive and forgive and forgive so they may begin again and again and again.... I wrapped myself around the girl as she climbed those stairs and prepared for the procedure. I stayed with her the whole time she was in that room and afterward. I watched from above and infused the room with peace. I brought the woman who placed the cloth over the girl's eyes and offered her a kind, gentle hand to hold. The assistant was going to take the day off because her grandchild was sick and both parents had to go to work that day. I prompted the neighbor to offer to sit with the child that day so that his grandmother could go to the clinic after all. I couldn't take away the physical pain of the girl's body or the emotional pain from her heart, but I blessed the girl's pain with purpose so that one day when she was ready, the girl could take this tragic moment and turn it into hope and help for the world. I hoped she would look back and feel that in her darkest hour I had held space for the light.

10

Re-Knowing Myself

"You are imperfect, you are wired for struggle, but you are worthy of love and belonging."
—Brene Brown

For too long I allowed myself to get so hung up on one single thing I had done unskillfully, that I forgot all the countless wonderful things I have done brilliantly. My first two years in the YOM program, I brushed off the month dedicated to self-love because *of course* I already loved myself. I casually did the self-love practices while I waited eagerly for the more "relevant" content that was to come. It was in my third year of YOM that a new idea began to dawn on me. Maybe self-love was more relevant than all the other topics combined. Maybe self-love was the key to unlocking everything else that I wanted in life. Could my disregard for the importance of actively practicing loving myself actually be an unconscious form of self-sabotage?

I realized that I needed to do some extra credit work to catch up on many years of ignoring myself. I mentally started listing out all the great facts and characteristics about me that I could think of. I flattered myself shamelessly and gave myself the biggest ego boost of my life: I'm a wonderful mom. I'm beautiful. I'm smart. I have a lovely singing voice. I'm patient, persistent, kind, compassionate, and driven. I have a natural gift for teaching English as a second language. I'm an exceptionally talented Pilates instructor. I love to serve others. I am a model ambassador of love.

As I scanned through all my wonderful characteristics, it felt great to recognize myself for being the awesome person I am. I had always thought that I shouldn't focus on my good qualities because it was conceited. Well, if not being conceited meant hating myself, then no thank you. I needed this boost in the self-esteem department. Listing my good qualities helped lift me up, but it also helped me notice where I still kept getting stuck. I knew that I was a wonderful mother, but I continued to judge myself for the one mistake I felt I had made as a mother. I needed to analyze this a bit further.

What are the qualities of a mother? A mother is loving and kind. She advocates for her children. She guides her children wisely and protects them at all costs. She's your hero. All these descriptions felt like me, but in my mind I still had evidence to prove otherwise. I ached to fit my "perfect" concept of a mother and nothing else. Once again I was throwing out all the times I had behaved like an "ideal mother" in favor of the one time I had deviated from that vision.

Have you ever heard the story of the two wolves? This story describes a Cherokee chief teaching his grandson a great lesson about life. He tells his grandson that inside every person a battle is raging between two wolves—a dark wolf, representing fear, anger, regret, despair, self-pity, etc., and a light wolf, representing love, empathy, hope, compassion, joy, etc. The boy naturally wonders which wolf will win. His grandfather wisely replies that the one he feeds will win.

Here I sat, consciously seeking evidence of my light wolf while subconsciously focusing on the actions of my dark wolf. I was still feeding the wrong one! Suddenly a memory leaped out at me. It was from my childhood, long before I ever had any children of my own, and yet it perfectly resonated with how I needed to see myself. Somehow it was appropriate that I have this memory from so long ago because it took place before I ever judged myself. It was like part of me was pleading, "Please look over here. This is your light wolf!" This memory is proof that I'm pretty amazing. I'll share this memory now as the epic story that it is when it plays out in my mind.

* * *

I was born and raised in California in the beautiful Central Coast area. Living amid this great beauty comes with a risk of peril because California is a place where earthquakes frequently occur. People who grow up in California are so used to them that we barely react if the ground shakes a little. Of course we practice earthquake drills in school. Everyone knows to "duck and cover" under shelter in an earthquake. We can all subconsciously spot the closest table or door frame and dive for safety in an instant.

One particular beautiful October afternoon, my best friend Shannon and her two younger sisters had all come over to our house after school. At one point my mom gathered us all in the living room to read to us for a while before she started dinner. My mom sat in a large chair with a gaggle of children gathered around her at her feet. Shannon's youngest sister was napping in my parents' bedroom just off the living room where the other seven of us sat. Shannon and I were each nine years old and the oldest of the group. My baby sister Irene was the youngest at eleven months old.

My mom read aloud from the book *Little Women* by Louisa May Alcott.

I held my baby sister in my lap so my mom could manage the book. I loved listening to stories and was in a half dream state. Shannon was less enchanted with the choice of book. She was bored out of her mind and could barely stay quiet or keep still.

The date was October 17, 1989, and the peaceful afternoon was about to erupt into chaos. Deep below us lay the living San Andreas fault, slowly but constantly moving and pressing with ever increasing intensity on the earth surrounding her. We didn't know it, but the fault had just reached the maximum amount of pressure it could sustain without shifting violently in its earthly bed. It was 5:04 in the evening.

Suddenly, an enormous jolt snapped me back to reality from my daydreams. The floor shook rapidly back and forth haphazardly, knocking us around and into each other. "EARTHQUAKE!" Shannon screamed over the sound of rumbling and booming. Everyone managed to pluck themselves off the floor and instinctively stumbled toward the kitchen on unsteady ground. Shannon reached the dining table and flung chairs out of the way to make room for everyone to shelter under it.

I was at the back of the pack. I still carried my sister in my arms. As I reached the kitchen, I witnessed the doors of our French door refrigerator fling themselves open and start heaving food recklessly onto the floor. This next bit I see in my mind as though it were a movie or a dream. All the audio stops. The frantic voices and rumbling walls are completely silent. I see the pitcher of orange juice in slow motion as it slides to the edge of the refrigerator shelf where it had been stored, and in the same moment loses its battle with equilibrium. The wet, shaking kitchen floor is like the surface of a slip-n-slide in a carnival fun house. I feel my feet shoot out from below me to the right as my body careens down like a felled tree to the left.

The noise comes back to my memory then. I somehow scrambled the rest of the way to the table on my knees, still carrying my baby sister.

The world continued to shake and roar for several more seconds, which felt more like minutes. I heard the china hutch crash over the dining table and the sound of glass shattering and raining down all around us. At some point while I crouched under the table my mom took Irene from my arms.

After some of the longest seconds of my life, it was all over. We all sat, stunned, for several more moments with big saucer eyes staring around in shocked silence. Did that really just happen? Was it really over? When we finally decided it was safe to emerge from our shelter, we saw a world torn apart. Everything that could shatter shattered. Everything that could fall fell over. Everything that wasn't anchored down moved. The china hutch now rested at a diagonal, supported only by the table that had protected us from serious injury. Every food and beverage stored in the refrigerator and freezer now lay in sloppy heaps on our kitchen floor. The upright piano had waltzed halfway across the living room. Shannon had to rescue her youngest sister from the bedroom where she had been napping because a bookshelf had fallen across the closed door, blocking easy access to the room.

The Loma Prieta earthquake, as it would be called, was the largest earthquake since the devastating San Francisco earthquake of 1906. It measured 6.9 on the Richter scale and lasted around 15 seconds. It was responsible for 63 deaths as well as thousands of injuries and massive destruction. Our family was quite lucky because the worst of our problems was that we had no water or electricity for several days afterwards.

As we assessed the damage around us, we examined ourselves as well. We suffered mostly bumps and bruises. I noticed I was cut on the outside of my left ankle from when I had slipped on the orange juice.

I didn't notice something until later when my mom mentioned it. She pointed out to me that I had protected my baby sister through all the chaos and pandemonium. Irene never hit the ground when I fell, as I ran with her to shelter. I have no idea how I pulled it off, but I remember cradling Irene protectively the whole time I carried her. Her head was to my left, the same direction that I fell. I distinctly recall a split second, when I knew I was going down, that I consciously maneuvered my body so that the back of my left shoulder would hit the ground, rather than the side or front where Irene's head was. I even remember lifting my left elbow up a bit as I smacked down on the linoleum floor, in order to absorb the impact for Irene. I couldn't have prepared for that fall, and yet I had naturally held Irene in just such a way as to keep her perfectly protected and safe. Maybe I'm just athletic. Maybe it was just good luck … or maybe I've always been a real life Superhero.

* * *

I could just have trusted in my capacity to be a loving and capable mother all along, but I didn't. Instead, I doubted myself until I could submit hard evidence. Fortunately, this Universe is kind, and it located a memory in which an act of nature forced me to prove my own capabilities to myself. In the end I don't have to look too much further than this memory to feed my light wolf. If indeed a mother is loving and kind, and protects her children at all costs, then I had already proven exactly who I was since before I started analyzing what any of it meant. No further evidence is required. This case is now closed.

If only proclaiming, "Case closed!" could actually settle the matter. Shifting my focus to look at my brilliance was the challenge all along, and part of me wanted to accept nothing less than full prosecution. Even with this amazing and true memory of my own heroism, I needed to figure out how to focus on it without dismissing it.

Intuitively I turned to meditation. My husband and I had taken a Transcendental Meditation® class in 2018, and since then I have practiced meditation daily. After my meditations—and sometimes completely separate from meditation—I would sit silently for a few minutes and turn my focus onto me. Mentally I began a process of stripping away everything I used to identify myself. For just a few minutes I set aside the fact that I'm a wife. I let go of the fact that I'm a mother. I released my attachment to inhabiting a female body. I set aside everything I could think of. I returned simply to being. As though from outside my body, I could see myself as just a soul. I think I started to get a sense of what the Creator feels when looking at me. When there was nothing left, I felt intense love for myself pouring in because there was no longer anything displacing it. Then, when I loved myself for no reason, I suddenly and simultaneously loved myself for every reason. I loved the perpetually scared little girl. I loved the preteen who lied about wanting her parents to visit her at science camp. I loved the teenager who had to push herself out of an unwanted embrace.... And I loved the young woman who had the abortion.

That year in YOM I saw the self-love practices in a new light. For the first time, I heard—*and understood*—that to love yourself you have to know yourself. For the first time in my life I worked on getting clear on who I am and realized I had had close to zero self-clarity. I had been defining myself in relation to other people—as a mother, a wife, a friend.... Those things were all lovely conditions, but I'm far greater than those conditions, and love is *unconditional*. This new understanding meant that I had to know myself on a deeper level. I had to figure out how to sit in a space where I loved myself just because.

Even though I practiced many of the same exercises that I had done in the previous two years in YOM, I felt a new sensation within my chest. It felt like my heart was breaking open and love was expanding inside me. I think Marci Shimoff would be proud to know that I (finally) took her advice. After three years in the YOM program and noticing and documenting all the ways that my life is amazing, I finally started seeing myself and truly believing that I, Elizabeth, am amazing.

I created the Unconditional Meditation for myself and for everyone holding this book. Please refer to the bonus content in the About the Author section at the end of the book for instructions on how to download it. I encourage everyone to do this meditation. Piece by piece, take away everything about you that comes to mind and sit in the empty space that remains. Find love in the nothing and allow it to flood and wash over you. Then fill yourself back up with everything—only I hope your lists of accolades grow much longer than mine originally did. Embellish and get creative. Be a monster-slaying superhero! This list is for your healing, which you deserve, and no one else needs to see it.

* * *

Let me take a brief moment here to acknowledge my mother who pointed out to me in the first place what I had done when I protected Irene. At the time, I was so focused on the shock of having just been through a massive earthquake, that I would have missed my valiant deed entirely. For all the times in my life when my mom may not have known how to support me, in this moment she lifted me up without even knowing the gift she was giving me. Thanks, Mom.

11

Climbing Mountains

> "The gem cannot be polished without friction, nor man perfected without trials."
> —Chinese Proverb

Metaphors abound in life. We see a rainbow after the rain and it reminds us that beauty follows a storm. We behold a grand tree that grew from a tiny seed and we know that deep within every human is unbounded potential. I enjoy noticing life's metaphors because they help me understand and appreciate life in meaningful and relatable ways.

Perhaps one of the most commonly referenced metaphors is that of a mountain representing a challenge. I personally have both compared and contrasted my healing journey with summiting a mountain on many occasions. It strikes me as a bit ironic that the grueling pain of healing from the trauma of abortion closely resembles an actual hobby of mine—hiking. At its most extreme, hiking can approach nearly unbearable levels of agony until reaching the highest point. I love hiking, but not because of the pain. I do it because I love the reward, and therefore the immense pleasure that results from a great hike is worth the pain.

CLIMBING MOUNTAINS

I begin a hike willingly, knowing more or less how long it will last and where it will lead me. I stop to take breaks if I need them, but the anticipation of reaching a summit with a glorious view spurs me on. I enjoy the nature I encounter along the way, and for the duration of the hike I know that I can turn around and go back at any time.

By contrast, the mountain that loomed ahead of me after having an abortion seemed foreboding and inhospitable, and I could not simply turn around and go back to the beginning of the trail. This mountain was completely uncharted. I had no idea how long the climb would take. The landscape appeared bleak and desolate. The journey felt depressing and lonely. I had no idea if I would ever reach the summit. I didn't know if there even was a summit. There was not much motivating me to move forward, but my options were limited because I had quite obviously crossed a point of no return. There was no going back to the beginning.

Despite the glaring differences between hiking and healing, it is actually the parallels between the two experiences that stand out the most for me. I'd like to share a particular hiking experience that most embodies my journey to healing. This story takes place in the summer of 2001. I had just completed an academic year abroad in Japan and was enjoying my last remaining weeks in that beautiful and amazing country.

**

When I was 21 I climbed Mount Fuji with a group of six close friends. The girl who organized the trip wanted to see the sun rise from the mountain's peak on her birthday. That meant we would climb overnight beginning the evening of July 13. We all carried backpacks stuffed with water, snacks, layers of clothing, and flashlights. We chose to hike from the Gotemba trail's fifth station. I'm not sure I knew at the time that

Gotemba is the lowest in altitude of the four fifth station locations on Mount Fuji. The Gotemba fifth station is located at nearly 4,600 feet. I did no research or training before undertaking this climb. I was young, fit, and full of enthusiasm. I was pretty sure those were the only qualities required to climb Japan's highest mountain.

At about 7:00 in the evening we set out on the path that began as a basic hike. It quickly became steeper, however, and the higher it got the colder the wind blew. While it was still light, we ascended above the tree line. Then the sun set. The biting chill of winter replaced the blazing hot summer weather we had left in the valley below. A large expanse of this section of trail is nothing but lava sand. For every painstaking step we took, we slid back half a step. Inevitably we had to take little breaks here and there from the grueling march to catch our breath and drink some water. Unfortunately, the unimpeded icy wind that blasted our sweaty bodies made us instantly too cold to stall for long. It became a game of choosing the lesser of two evils—take a much needed rest and freeze, or push ourselves past the boundary of our physical limits and stay warm.

Around the seventh station, at just over 9,000 feet in elevation, a couple of my companions started to complain of headaches and dizziness. The final stretch of the hike taxed all my strength and willpower. The rocks became like a giant's staircase—far enough apart that I had to rely on my upper body strength to help haul myself up. At this point I had to stop to catch my breath nearly every minute.

At 3:00 a.m. we summited Mount Fuji, some 12,300 feet above sea level and the highest point in Japan. It had taken eight grueling hours. Now that we had finally arrived at our highly anticipated destination ... we waited. Sunrise on the peak was still a cold, dark hour and a half away. My group huddled together in a circle wedged into a rocky outcropping on the exposed, wind-whipped peak of the iconic Mount Fuji. Exhausted and beyond cold, I tried not to cry.

Finally my prayer for warmth was answered when a restaurant hut opened maybe half an hour before sunrise. People swarmed in to warm themselves with hot food and shelter. Soon a pink light began to illuminate the eastern sky. It spread and its color deepened. We braved the cold once again to find the best view of one of nature's greatest shows. Suddenly one of my friends pointed. I looked to see a red arch peering over Earth's edge. The orb rose quickly as I gazed from my vantage point on the rooftop of Japan. The breathtaking feat of nature drew tears to my eyes as I realized we had spent eight hours climbing a cold, steep mountain for precisely this experience. We did it!

* * *

Had I fully known what to expect while summiting Mount Fuji, I honestly may never have attempted it. Equally, if I had understood even an inkling of how an abortion would tear me apart, I could never have gone through with it. These were two very different events with very different outcomes, but they both required one identical choice— do it. Once I made a decision to climb the mountain, I set an entire chain of events into motion. It grew in mass and gained momentum until it would have required more effort to stop it than to continue forward. At any point on the slope of Mount Fuji I could have turned around and returned to comfort. The journey still would have been dark and cold, if a little less arduous. The funny thing is I don't remember having thoughts of turning around. At a certain point I had invested so much into this journey that a mountaintop sunrise seemed more valuable than my own comfort.

Unlike climbing Mount Fuji, I had no idea as to the chasm of desolation that awaited me on the other side of an abortion. All I knew is that I was scared of how others might judge me if I became a mother at the age of 19. I thought if I outran my fears they might disappear.

With ignorance and fear as my guides, I plunged forward before I could think it through. I didn't want to know the truth. Isn't that the real tragedy? Deep down I knew the right answer was to allow myself to be the mother to my child, but I wanted to take action before my mind could catch up with my heart. I just didn't know that an abortion would create something far more formidable than a mountain.

Grief is a mountain. You know you have to scale it, but you don't always know where to start or how long it will take. You make lots of great strides forward only to slip back down drastically and unexpectedly. Sometimes for all the effort you put in, it feels like you're getting no return. You may have moments when you feel ill-equipped, beaten up, and weighed down with rocks in your shoes. Mount Fuji is an amazing metaphor that has helped me through my grief journey. It taught me several lessons.

First I learned that every half slide backward is actually a half step forward. During a healing process it's way too easy to see any regression and not notice the progress. It's just a matter of perspective or semantics, but I actually have to acknowledge these incredibly frustrating backslides as forward progress because, in the end, I still arrived where I wanted to go.

Second, I realized that half steps are sufficient to get you to the top. I wish I could have taken large, confident strides toward my goal without losing any ground. I couldn't ... and yet I still made it.

Third, I learned that when it reaches the coldest and darkest point, things can only get warmer and brighter. Unfortunately, with grief there's no way to know when you've arrived at the worst point. That's why at this stage it feels the easiest to give up or pointless to continue and requires the most faith and hopefully some outside help.

Fourth, I found out that a sunrise at the top of a mountain is only a bonus. The sunrise is not the reward itself. Granted, it's a very well-packaged bonus, but take a look at where you are and realize how you got there. Give credit where credit is due and pat yourself on the back. Then enjoy the dazzling gift provided courtesy of Mother Nature. This concept of self appreciation naturally led me to one more realization which is ...

Fifth, and most importantly, the real gift is myself. The fact is that I am capable of facing a challenge as big as a mountain, tackling it, and making it to the other side. I went through an incredible process and am better for it. I am naturally stronger for having heaved myself up and over every boulder in my path. I am wiser for having learned my way up to the peak. Looking out from the uppermost point, I can both feel and know that I mastered this mountain.

There is no right way to climb a mountain. Pick a side, choose a trail, and start walking. The truth is that the sun will always rise. You get to decide if you'll look or not and you get to choose your vantage point.

12

Grace

"I do not at all understand the mystery of grace—only that it meets us where we are but does not leave us where it found us."
—Anne Lamott

I have to acknowledge that something massive was at play during my healing years. It was something so amazing that it allowed me to feel peace even after suffering for so long. It doesn't make any sense logically because I can't change the past, so my error still exists. If my error still exists, how can I truly feel at ease, no matter how many hindsight stories I write? I can only describe this phenomenon of healing when it didn't seem possible as "grace." Grace is a concept known in many religions of the world, but I most intimately understand it through the lens of Christianity in which I was raised. Christians describe grace as a gift that God gives to people unexpectedly, even though they don't deserve it. I don't think religion is required to understand grace. Haven't you ever experienced a child throwing a temper tantrum or otherwise behaving badly? Did you or the parent give the child the grace of forgiveness for the poor behavior without holding it against the child for the rest of her life? That's how humans demonstrate grace to each other. When we let go of something in order to move on, we give the gift of grace.

Reflecting back, I see how grace has always surrounded me, even and especially in my darkest days and lowest circumstances. To fall so far as to end all potential for my child's life and then to learn how to grow wings and soar above the pain is nothing short of grace. For me it was a huge mistake to have an abortion, and that made it hard for me to see the possibility of receiving any forgiveness, compassion, or help for mending my error. Grace found me anyway.

Grace occurs because of love. We are all made of love and therefore we can't escape it. Love is our true nature. Even when we defy who we are, love is always there, in the form of grace, ready to lift us up as soon as we're ready to receive it. Grace in action is the rainbow after the storms of our lives. It is releasing judgment. It is seeing the value in a mistake, learning from it, and making higher choices next time. Grace is releasing the past in order to create the space for what is to come.

Do you have sufficient grace around your emotions? For a long time I didn't. With all emotions, we must have the grace to release them after we have experienced them and processed their meaning. I held onto misery, hoping that it would never die. I refused for ages to allow it to cycle naturally through me. I may as well have been eating out of the compost heap. An apple past its prime, though once healthy, becomes unfit for human consumption. As it withers, it is useless and even harmful inside the human body. In one sense old produce (like a negative emotion) seems worthless, yet put it in the right place, and it has the power to alchemize itself and enrich soil. It helps create the perfect conditions for new healthy growth to occur again.

Incidentally, this only happens out in the open air. No, you don't have to announce your abortion to the whole world. You just have to stop hiding from it and instead take responsibility for it. When we discard our food "trash" into plastic bags, we hide it which cuts off the oxygen supply, thus preventing the proper breakdown of materials. Sure, we can't see the ugliness anymore, but it will still be there, stifled and stinking, if we ever decide to dig it up. Throw that same food "trash" into the dirt, mix it up, and expose it to air instead, and in time all you'll see is rich, healthy soil with new life growing out of it.

Every ripe, juicy apple that I bite is possible because an old, decaying apple was allowed to decompose in the earth. As I enjoy the fruit, I never mourn the loss of the previous apples. I never feel appalled that they had to get ugly and rotten. Why not? It's because the present is the only thing that matters. I enjoy the ripe fruit that I eat now because that's what serves me. The past doesn't matter. Clinging to its memory only keeps me a prisoner to the decay which has no place inside a living, thriving human.

I thought my pain was shameful, worthless trash. I totally missed the value of facing the pain and trudging through the muck. Thankfully, grace is patient. When I finally dug up all the garbage, it was there waiting for me, just as awful and stinking as I expected it to be. Despite neglecting my trash for so long, though, it was no less ready to be worked and transformed into something wonderful, new, and perfect. So far, the muck has become a book and a quilt. That is more than enough, but what else may come, I wonder, if I keep working?

My own unborn baby helped me in the most improbable of ways. The pain and shame I felt from choosing abortion was there not to torture me, but to show me that I had some big work to do. I could have chosen to have my baby. I would have loved my child and appreciated my life, but I never would have known the depth of my own love. The contrast of losing what we love the most is the strongest way to know that love. We only appreciate light because we know darkness. If the same side of the earth always faced the sun, would we feel grateful for its light or completely take it for granted? I'm not saying that I had to have an abortion to know that I love my child, but the depth of that love drove me to do work I never would have undertaken under other circumstances. The work I did showed me how to love *myself*. Through the pain of loss I was forced to choose healing or die trying.

When I had no idea what to do to heal, I grasped at straws and tried anything I could get my hands on. The memory of someone I had never met, but whom I desperately wanted to know, both tortured me and urged me on. For the better part of two decades I felt haunted by my daughter, as though she were somewhere close, just out of view. I often had visions of her at the age she would actually be if she were alive now. It's through my desire to know my unborn daughter that I sought abortion recovery support, studied miracles, and wrote a book. In everything I did I kept trying to know my child. I named her and wrote her several letters over the years. I had entire conversations with her in my mind. I made the baby quilt for her even though it would never keep her sleeping body warm. I did all these things because I was trying to have a daughter whom I had lost. Contrary to what I thought, however, through all the letter writing, conversations, and quilt making, I slowly learned that my child was not lost at all. I never would have done all those things for no reason. My child was so close that she filled me and surrounded me showing me not only who she was, but who I am—creative, strong, resilient, loving, and worthy of love. What I discovered is that when I finally knew myself I knew my child, too.

I realized that my child's gifts are the lessons she has been teaching me all these years. She helped me remember that love and forgiveness are my birthright. Love and forgiveness are things that all humans can never be without even when we would try to fool ourselves. Judging others or judging ourselves makes us feel like we have effectively separated the person from the love. We do this all the time, but how silly this notion is! Love can only be love if it's unconditional. That means that we love *no matter what*. We don't have to love a person's actions to love the person. Right next to love, as its loyal companion, stands forgiveness ever by its side. In the moment when I decided that I hated my abortion, I tried to place myself outside the bounds of love and forgiveness. The impossibility of this separation made it very difficult for me to feel comfortable with love again. It made the work feel harder and the obstacles appear bigger. Fortunately, all that big work brought me back to a place of harmony within myself, where I could exist both as the one who chose abortion *and* as the one who loves her anyway.

Making a mistake is never wrong. It is especially wonderful when we can come full circle with a mistake, from occurrence to judgment to forgiveness. My healing journey was a valuable experience because it taught me that I was already forgiven before I ever made any mistake. Forgiveness is automatically linked to every misstep, not so that we can proceed as though nothing ever happened, but so that we can proceed with the knowledge of what happened and the wisdom to choose differently the next time. In this way we carry on, always forward in our lives, striving to make our clumsy strides ever more graceful.

If I had had a baby daughter when I was 19, I almost certainly would have named her Tatiana. It's an elegant and cute name and one that I still like. One of the most interesting aspects about my particular journey is that I named a child who is not physically present. Her name is precious, but it only matters to me. It doesn't matter to her or to anyone else. One day in the spring of 2021, I enjoyed a moment to myself following a meditation, and I thought about my daughter. In quiet contemplation, a sense of clarity and knowing filled me. Somehow an energetic shift occurred within me, and it felt like I finally synched up with the vibration of the being who would have been my child. I felt so much peace around the thought of her that I knew she was with me even though I couldn't see, hear, or touch her. As a wave of gentle joy washed over me, I somehow "heard" my daughter tell me her name. I felt my daughter's sweet, gentle presence fill me and surround me, and I laughed to myself. "Of course," I thought. It's not that I had given her the wrong name in the first place, but I had imbued the name Tatiana with the heaviness that I had carried around with my thoughts of her for years. My daughter's spirit is the opposite of heavy. It's light and carefree. I feel lighter, too, now that I finally call my child by the name that she revealed. Her name is Grace.

It is through both my child Grace and the mystery of grace that I forgave myself and made peace with my past. I worked hard to achieve forgiveness when I thought I didn't deserve it. When I finally found forgiveness, it was a relief to know it had always been there.

To do something that doesn't align with our true nature is sometimes part of our human experience, and it can feel awful and devastating. Those awful feelings aren't there to torture us, but to remind us that we have work to do to re-balance ourselves. We can take comfort in knowing that support is all around us, and a variety of tools are at our disposal to help us return to inner harmony. If you are experiencing heartache and suffering after an abortion, please know that healing lies somewhere between grief and action, so get going, one prayer, one quilt, and one hindsight story at a time. Believe that the healing you seek is already yours. It's only a matter of you grasping and accepting it in a way that makes sense to you. As you work to close the gap between the misstep and the healing, you'll discover that from this point through the rest of your life, every single time you misstep, you are already forgiven.

Afterword

"Your task is not to seek for love, but merely to seek and find all the barriers within yourself that you have built against it."
—Rumi

One of the biggest ways I have ever deceived myself as a parent, a partner, and as a friend is in thinking that I could love another person more than I love myself. It's not possible. It's a nice sounding little lie that made me feel good about myself while not requiring me to do any work toward improving myself. I thought I needed one thing—a relationship with my baby. The power of grace knew that I needed so much more. I would have limited myself, but this benevolent Universe guided me, kicking and stumbling, to something much better, more complete, and more fulfilling—a more deeply evolved relationship with the person I need to love the most—myself.

I think Michelangelo would agree that everyone who seeks healing is already healed. We are both the artist and the block of marble. Whatever we declare is hidden inside that rock is truly there, but it is up to us to be the sculptor who can painstakingly carve it out bit by bit and in the right proportions with just the right amount of angles, curves, and jagged lines.

The most important thing I ever learned on my journey from grief to grace is that I am the master. I am in charge. It's strange because while the actual healing occurred in a single moment, in another very real sense it took me over two decades to decide I was finally okay. Then

AFTERWORD

again, that was the key all along—I had to *decide* I was finally okay. Until I changed my thinking I was never going to feel whole again.

Today I am healed because I make a decision every day to be healed. Everything in life is a choice, including the way I feel about myself and my past decisions. While today it's extremely rare that I feel emotionally triggered by the memory of my abortion, I still have challenging days and low moments as a natural course of life. Those are the times when it's easier to get knocked off balance and slip into grief.

I remember how sometimes on my abortion anniversary or due date anniversary I used to find myself walking the narrow path of emotional balance which I imagine is not unlike crossing a high wire strung across a gorge. One wobble or misstep plunged me into the gaping abyss of despair. My body still has memories of a pain too long carried and sometimes the old pathways seem far too familiar. For a long time I found it crucial to walk an emotional tightrope. (It's a skill I don't recommend developing.) More importantly, though, I learned to cross the chasm and step back onto the solid ground of love. This is my true path. Yes, I still make missteps, but when I notice them I quickly correct my course.

When I started writing, my memorial baby quilt was still unfinished. With the help of my mother-in-law, Marge, I pulled the quilt out of storage and assessed the progress. It lacked only the binding. I bought fabric, borrowed Marge's sewing machine, and finished the baby quilt 15 years after starting it. It was worth the wait. Also it was another miracle. The completion of the quilt did, in fact, coincide with my healing.

"Help me release that which no longer serves." In my own prayer I acknowledged that I could not heal alone. Here I have released my story as words that drained out of my body and poured into the pages of a book. Thank you to everyone who has read these words because you aid me in my healing journey and in the collective healing journey of everyone. Every word that is read is cleansed. I therefore release this book to the world in the name of love. All stuck emotions, I command you to go forth now, out of my body and on to your next expression. You are free. I am free.

Grace's Quilt

Resources

While this is not an exhaustive list, these are some resources that I personally found to be highly valuable when I earnestly began the healing work:

- Your Year of Miracles https://youryearofmiracles.com/mp/join/
- Marci Shimoff https://happyfornoreason.com/
- Dr. Sue Morter https://drsuemorter.com/
- Paul Selig https://paulselig.com/
- Transcendental Meditation https://www.tm.org/

About the Author

Elizabeth Boyd was born and raised in Hollister, California. She has a degree in international studies from the Middlebury Institute of International Studies at Monterey, and is a certified Romana's Pilates® instructor. Elizabeth moved with her family from the United States to Portugal, following a dream to live in Europe. A passionate world traveler, Elizabeth has lived in Thailand and Japan and has traveled through many countries in Southeast and East Asia and the European Mediterranean. In addition to travel, Elizabeth enjoys fitness, meditation, writing, and being a mother.

* * *

Connect

To learn more about Elizabeth or for information on upcoming courses, please visit lotusleaper.com or send an email to Elizabeth@lotusleaper.com.

* * *

Bonus Content

As a thank you for reading this book, please download a copy of Elizabeth's "Unconditional Meditation" at lotusleaper.com/unconditional-meditation.

www.ingramcontent.com/pod-product-compliance
Lightning Source LLC
Chambersburg PA
CBHW070854050426
42453CB00012B/2193